Cartoons

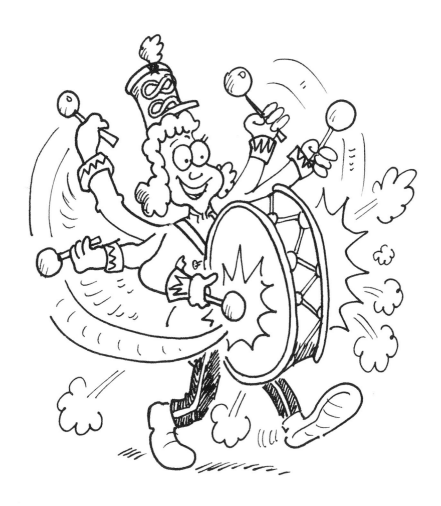

JOHN BYRNE

If you have enjoyed *Learn to Draw Cartoons*, why not consider putting your skills to good use? John Byrne's *Drawing Cartoons That Sell* is available from HarperCollins*Publishers*, priced £7.99. ISBN 0 00 710538 X.

HarperCollins*Publishers*
77-85 Fulham Palace Road
Hammersmith
London W6 8JB

The HarperCollins website address is
www.**fire**and**water**.com

Collins is a registered trademark of
HarperCollins*Publishers*

02 04 06 07 05 03 01
8 10 12 14 13 11 9

© HarperCollins*Publishers* 1995

Editor: Diana Craig
Art Director: Pedro Prá-Lopez, Kingfisher Design Services
DTP/Typesetting: Frances Prá-Lopez, Kingfisher Design Services
Contributing artists: John Clube, Joel Mischon, Janet Nunn

A catalogue record for this book is available from the British Library

ISBN 0 00 413354 4

Printed by Midas Printing, Hong Kong

CONTENTS

Introduction

I've been drawing cartoons for as long as I can remember. And for as long as I can remember, people have been looking over my shoulder and saying, 'I wish I could do that.'

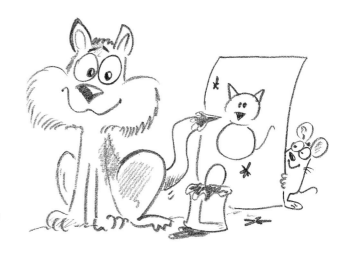

Well, the good news is that everyone *can* learn to draw cartoons. I've taught hundreds of people from a wide variety of backgrounds, most of whom were convinced that they 'couldn't draw a straight line'. Guess what? Many of them still can't ... but it hasn't stopped them drawing some great cartoons and having a lot of fun in the process. You see, the nice thing about cartoons is that they are *supposed* to look funny.

We won't be using very many straight lines in the following pages, but I will show you how to build up a whole cartoon world from a few basic shapes (most of which you can probably draw already). I've done lots of cartoons and step-by-step instructions to give you ideas, and you'll be surprised at how much your work will improve with a little practice.

Another nice thing about learning to draw cartoons is that even the 'homework' is fun: use this book as your starting point, but try to collect as many other cartoons as you can. You'll laugh a lot and also learn a lot by seeing how different cartoonists put the techniques in this book into practice – and, before you know it, you'll have developed your own unique and recognizable style of cartoon drawing.

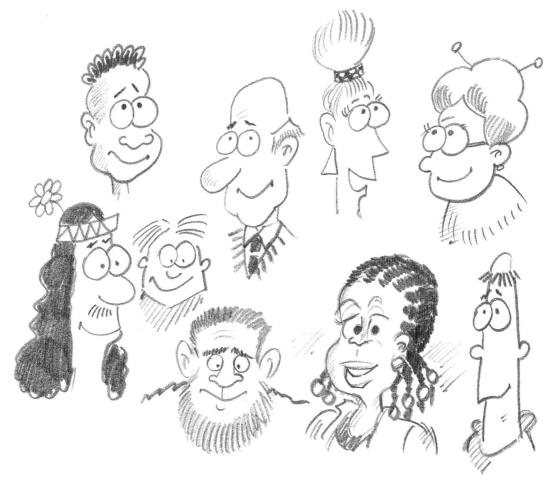

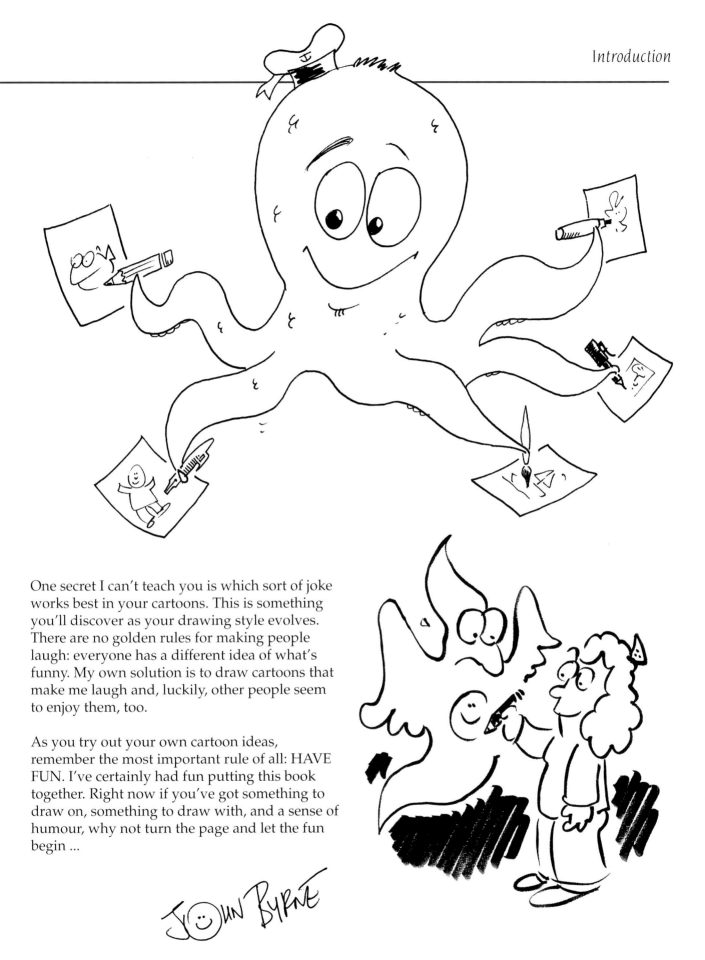

One secret I can't teach you is which sort of joke works best in your cartoons. This is something you'll discover as your drawing style evolves. There are no golden rules for making people laugh: everyone has a different idea of what's funny. My own solution is to draw cartoons that make me laugh and, luckily, other people seem to enjoy them, too.

As you try out your own cartoon ideas, remember the most important rule of all: HAVE FUN. I've certainly had fun putting this book together. Right now if you've got something to draw on, something to draw with, and a sense of humour, why not turn the page and let the fun begin ...

JOHN BYRNE

Tools and Equipment

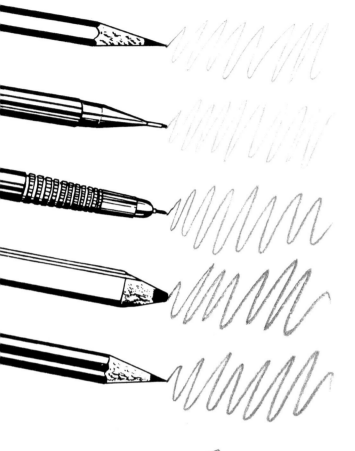

Pencils

One of the most versatile of all drawing tools, pencils come in many different varieties, each giving your finished cartoon a different effect.

Pencils are categorized according to hardness of lead. A 9H pencil, the hardest, gives a sharp, thin line, while a 9B, the softest, produces a line that is much thicker and darker. Many cartoonists use a 2B or 3B pencil to give a good, strong line for finished drawings. A 2H pencil is ideal for light preliminary sketches which you can go over later with ink, felt-tip pen, or a darker pencil.

A wide range of coloured pencils is also available, including some which can be applied to the paper, then moistened to give a watercolour effect.

If you want to keep your pencil drawings looking their best, spray them with fixative to preserve them – the B pencils are especially prone to smudging.

The soft outlines of a 3B pencil are especially useful when creating furry cartoon characters.

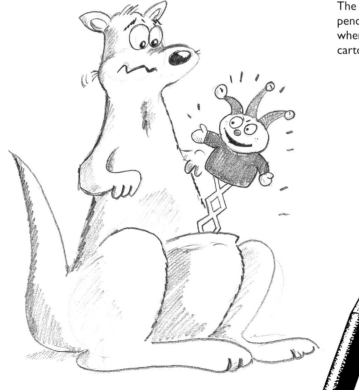

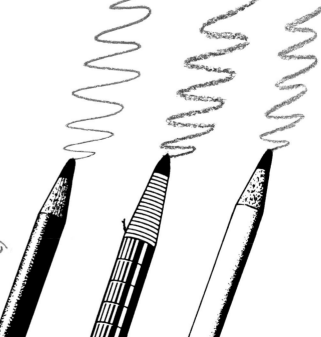

Wax crayon

Cheap, easy to grip – and next to impossible to do really precise drawings with – wax crayons are an ideal medium to try if you're having trouble loosening up your drawing style. Get the biggest, chunkiest crayon you can find and go wild!

Charcoal and conté crayon

Once you've experimented with crayon, you might like to try charcoal and conté sticks. Both give a very strong, dark line, which is ideal for cartoons; the disadvantage is that they also break and smudge very easily – but where's the fun of being a cartoonist if you can't make a mess? (Do spray on some fixative if you want to display your masterpieces later on.)

One of my favourite loosening up exercises: I give myself a child's crayon and a few minutes to see how many activities I can get my cartoon character to perform. As you can see, energy is much more important than accuracy of drawing.

Artist's Tip

You can cut down on smudging by placing a piece of paper under your hand as you draw. Your hands will stay cleaner, too!

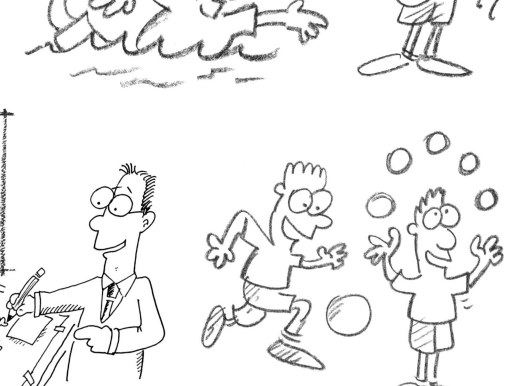

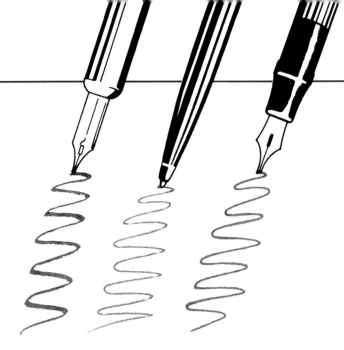

Pens

Many cartoonists choose pen as their favourite medium. There are many different types of pen, and you'll probably experiment with quite a few before you find the one that best suits your particular style. I've tried a great variety over the years, but now my favourite pen travels with me everywhere.

Ballpoint is the sort of pen most of us start doodling with. Ballpoint pens are cheap and handy to have around for sketches and detail, but their rigid point and unchanging line is mainly designed for writing and doesn't lend itself to producing lively cartoons. Ballpoints also clog and smudge easily. On the other hand, they don't dry up if you leave the top off – a big advantage if you're as absent-minded as me!

Technical drawing pens produce a good black line, which never varies in width. This is good news for architects who have to produce neat, precise drawings, but less useful for cartoonists. The lack of flexibility of these pens makes them more suitable for technical tasks – such as drawing the boxes around comic strips – rather than drawing the cartoons themselves. Technical pens do come in a range of different widths, however, so you can create interesting effects by using a number of different pen widths on the same cartoon.

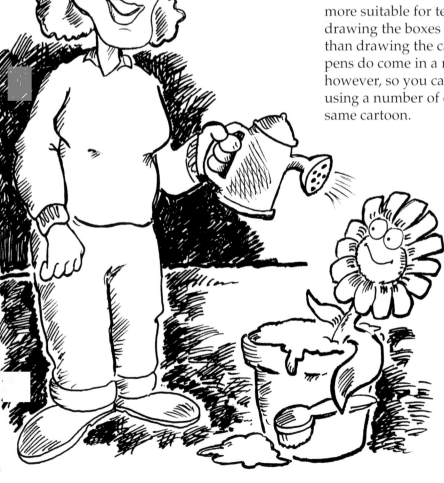

You can add detail to a simple pen cartoon by 'cross-hatching' – overlapping lots of small pen strokes to create dark tones and shadows.

Fountain pens offer a variety of different nibs in different shapes. Experiment with them to see which best suits you. By altering your pressure on the nib, you can produce a lively line which varies in thickness at different points. Some artists still prefer the old-fashioned dip pen, but many of the newer pens can be loaded with ink cartridges, giving the convenience of a constant, flowing line without the necessity of having to refill every few minutes.

Marker pens are available in a number of different forms, from inexpensive packs for children to professional pens in hundreds of colours. Hard fibre-tip pens give a thin line suitable for the drawing of details. On the other hand, wide felt-tip pens are a good tool for adding large flat areas of colour to your finished cartoons.

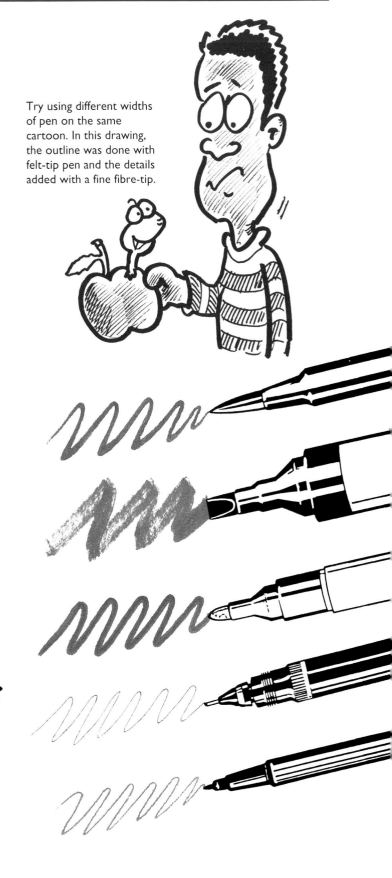

Try using different widths of pen on the same cartoon. In this drawing, the outline was done with felt-tip pen and the details added with a fine fibre-tip.

Using square-tipped markers or a calligraphy pen makes for interesting line drawings.

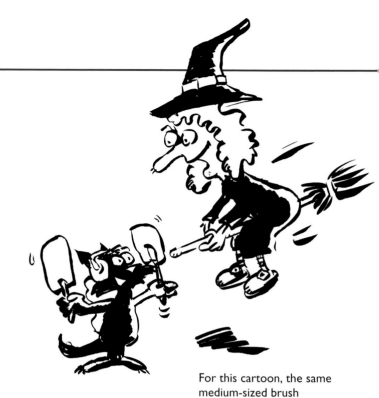

Brushes and wet media

For every cartoonist who favours pen and ink, there's another who swears that brush gives a far more expressive line. Of course, there are quite a few who use both, and you will enjoy experimenting with the wide variety of brushes available. You'll find very small ones for fine details, and much wider brushes which will allow you to fill in large solid areas of black or colour quickly.

Dry brush gives cartoons a 'sophisticated' look favoured by upmarket magazine cartoonists – but this look is, in fact, very simple to achieve. Load your brush with ink and then allow it partially to dry on a sheet of blotting paper before applying the brush to your cartoon.

Ink may be diluted to produce a wash drawing, adding grey tones to your cartoon.

Watercolour may be a little too 'soft' a medium for most cartoons, but watercolour paints and coloured inks can certainly brighten up your finished drawings.

For this cartoon, the same medium-sized brush allowed me to produce thick and thin strokes, as well as solid black areas.

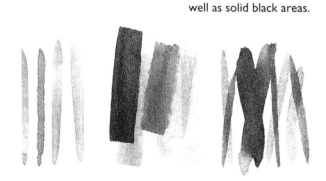

These marks were made with *(from left to right)* a small, pointed brush; a flat brush; a large, pointed brush.

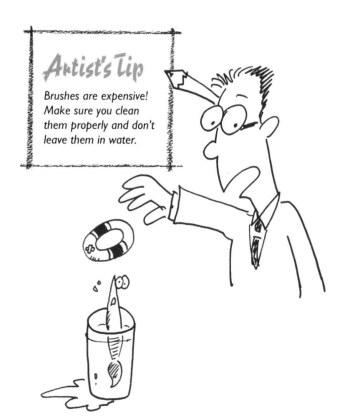

Artist's Tip

Brushes are expensive! Make sure you clean them properly and don't leave them in water.

For an even layer of strong watercolour, add darker washes to a light wash while still wet.

To prevent colours 'bleeding' together, let the first wash dry before adding the next.

Instant tone

You can buy sheets of adhesive instant tone in a variety of different textures and dot patterns. It gives finished cartoons a very professional 'printed' look, but is best used sparingly – not least because it can be quite expensive.

The method shown below makes the most of this mechanical tone with the least amount of wastage. When cutting out the tone with a knife or blade, always take great care that you don't cut yourself, too – dried blood is one of my least favourite media!

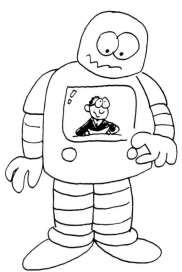

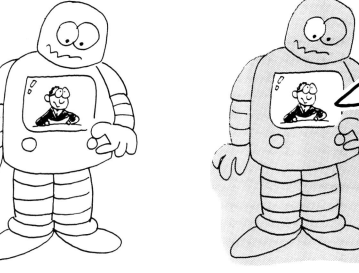

3 Carefully trim away excess tone with a scalpel or craft knife. Be careful not to cut through the drawing paper. Save the excess pieces of tone on the backing paper that comes with the sheet and use it for other cartoons.

1 Draw your cartoon with pen or brush.

2 Cut out and stick down a piece of tone slightly bigger than your cartoon *(left)*.

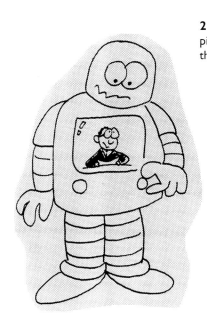

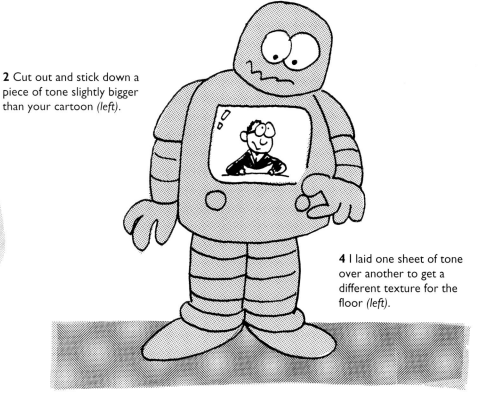

4 I laid one sheet of tone over another to get a different texture for the floor *(left)*.

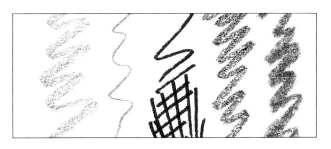

Newsprint is very inexpensive, which makes it good for practising and rough sketching.

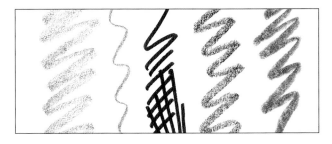

Tracing paper is semi-transparent, so that you can lay it over other images and trace them.

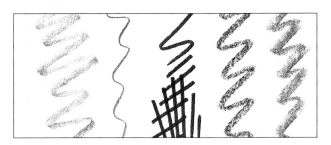

Stationery paper, usually available in one size, has a hard, smooth surface that works well with pen.

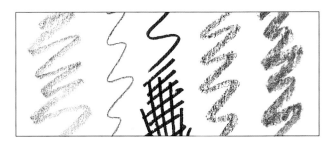

Cartridge paper usually has a slightly textured surface, and is one of the most versatile surfaces.

Surfaces to draw on

Drawing on the right type of paper can make a big difference to the look of your finished cartoon – but getting hold of the right quantity of paper is even more important. Cartoonists go through huge amounts of paper, and the more you can recycle the better it will be for the environment, and for your pocket. You'll certainly need lots of rough paper for all the sketches, doodles, trial runs and flashes of inspiration you'll come up with on the way to your finished masterpieces.

Offcuts are quantities of paper left over from odd-sized print jobs which can often be had cheaply or even free. Ask your local printer or newspaper office.

Lining paper is another option if you want cheap paper in large quantities. Rolls of lining paper are also inexpensive and can be bought from wallpaper and decorating stores.

Newsprint comes in large sheets, and is inexpensive, but be wary of pen and marker 'bleeding' through the paper and spoiling the sheet underneath. Newsprint eventually turns yellow, so it's not ideal if you want to preserve your best work for posterity.

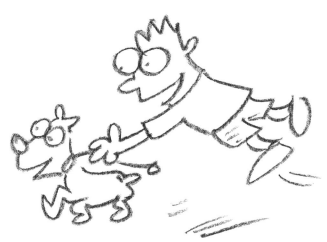

The surface of cartridge paper has a slight roughness which helps to emphasize the grainy texture of crayon, as in this quick cartoon *(above)*.

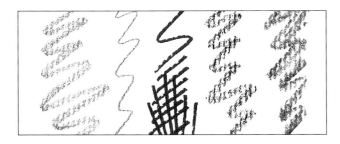

Ingres paper, in various colours and with a lightly ridged surface, is ideal for pastel and charcoal.

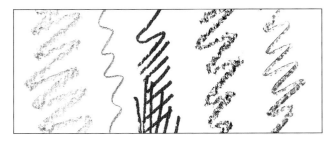

Watercolour paper is thick and absorbent, and has a rough surface. It is good for wet media.

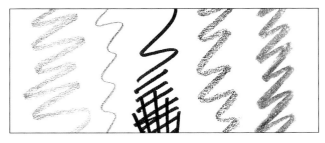

Bristol board is stiff and has a smooth finish that makes it a good surface for pen drawings.

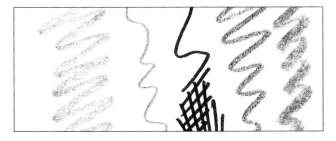

Layout paper is a semi-opaque, lightweight paper that is most suitable for pen or pencil drawings.

Typing paper is used by many professionals for finished cartoons. You can buy it cheaply and in large quantities, A4 (297 x 210 in) being the most popular size. Heavier-quality paper gives a good, smooth surface for drawing in pen or pencil, while the lighter papers are semi-transparent and useful for tracing.

Bristol board is a light, white board particularly popular with strip cartoonists as it takes detailed brush or pen work equally well.

Cartridge papers have various surface textures which can bring out the characteristics of pencils, crayons and charcoal, while drawing on coloured papers can produce unusual effects.

I drew this cartoon with white ink on black paper to make the prison cell look even gloomier.

The caption to this cartoon could read: *'Today's horoscope: you need to get out more often.'*

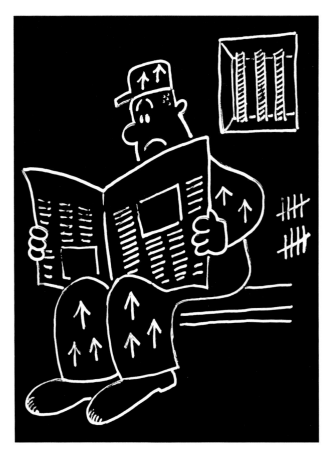

Choosing the Right Medium

Each cartoonist tries to create a style that is unique and individual. How you draw affects the way your finished cartoons look, but the tools you use and the surface on which you use them also play a part.

The transformation on these two pages was achieved with the help of a full moon – and a number of different media. Sometimes the effect is stark and simple, ideal for topical, political cartoons. Some media are capable of showing lots of detail, which would work well for a comic strip adventure, while other tools give a soft edge which might suit a children's book or a humorous birthday card.

Try different combinations on one of your own cartoons – with a little practice, you'll be able to choose the right tools for the job every time.

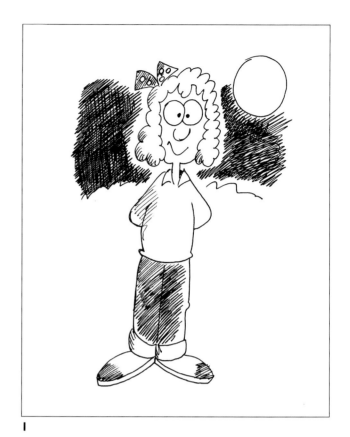

1

2

1 Ballpoint on light cartridge paper
2 Brush and ink wash on typing paper
3 Soft pencil on textured cartridge paper
4 Dip pen with a fine nib on card
5 Hard pencil on tracing paper
6 Calligraphy felt tip on heavy cartridge paper

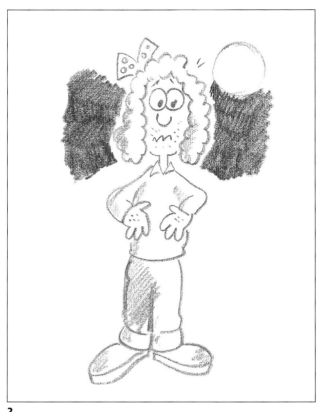

3

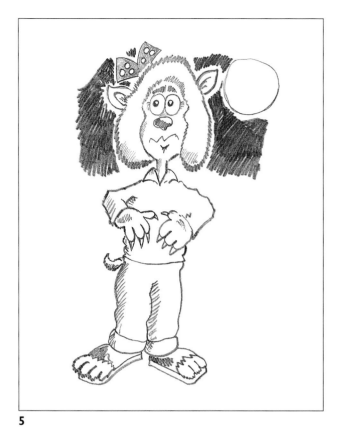

5

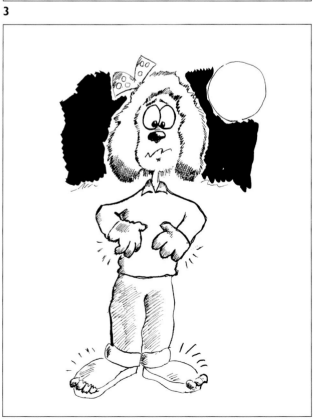

4

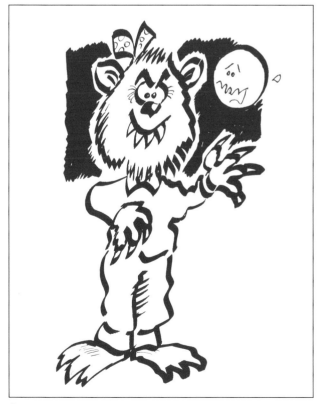

6

Basic Shapes

Drawing any figure, from a cartoon character to the Mona Lisa, can be a bit daunting if you try to do it all in one go – but build your figure up from simple shapes and the job becomes a lot easier.

Take a look at some cartoon characters from newspapers, books or television. What basic shapes do you think the artist used to draw these cartoons? Can you make your own, different characters from the same shapes?

Keep it light
When putting together your own basic shapes, don't worry if your circles and ovals don't look exactly the same as mine. They are guidelines to help you draw your finished picture. Draw them lightly in pencil, so you can play around with them as much as you want before drawing over them to create your finished cartoon.

You'll enjoy cartooning much more and produce much nicer-looking cartoons if you can learn to draw with an easy, flowing line. Doing light preliminary drawings will help you relax when you are doing your final drawing. Remember also that big shapes are much easier to draw. Give yourself plenty of space and try to fill the whole page with your cartoon.

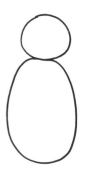

1 Which bit of the body you start with depends on you. I usually begin with a large oval shape for the torso, and then add a smaller circle for the head.

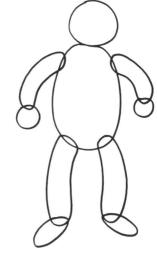

2 I then add 'sausages' for the arms and legs, with some smaller ovals and sausages on the ends for hands and feet.

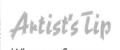

Artist's Tip

When you first start drawing like this, you may have trouble with arms and legs going off the page. Drawing your basic figure in very light pencil at first will help solve this problem.

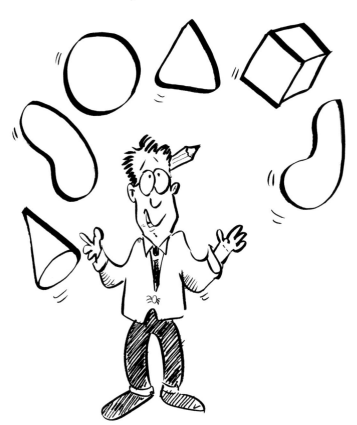

Almost everyone can already draw simple circles and ovals, triangles and squares like these, so once you've practised drawing a few of the all-important 'sausages', you'll have all the tools you need to begin.

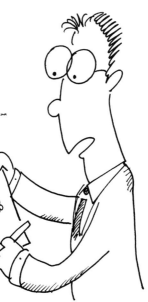

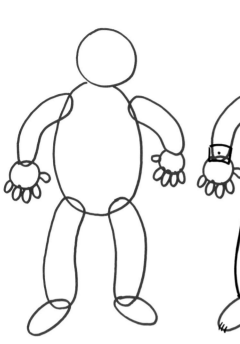

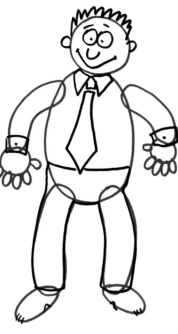

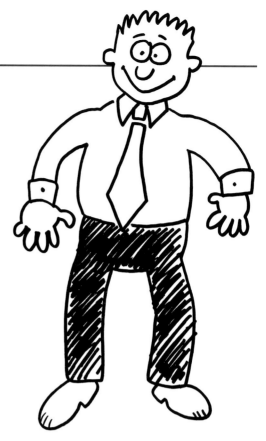

3 Add some fingers and you now have a basic figure shape to which you can add hair, facial features and clothes.

4 Draw the preliminary figure in pencil. When you've added all the extra bits, only ink over the lines you want to keep in your cartoon.

5 Any remaining pencil construction lines can be rubbed out.

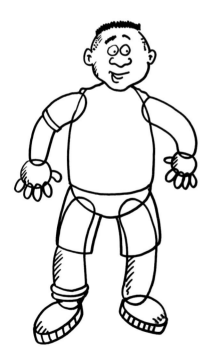

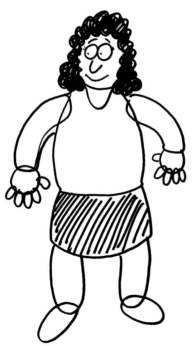

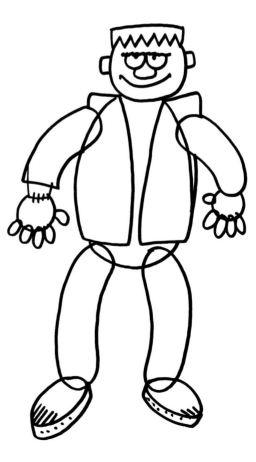

Using the same figure, practise turning it into different characters.

Drawing Animals

Drawing animals

The same shapes we've used for people can be used for animals, too. With one or two simple additions you can create a whole menagerie of cartoon creatures.

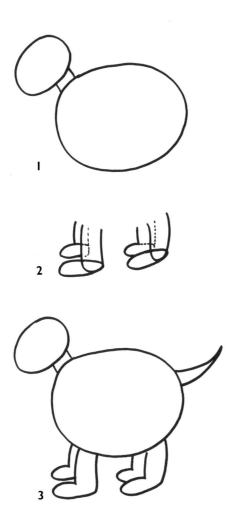

1 To draw a basic animal body, use the same shapes you used for humans.

2 Leaving the legs on the far side incomplete makes them look further away.

3 Don't forget the tail!

Adding whiskers, collars, horns and hooves to your basic shape turns it into these three very different animals *(right)*.

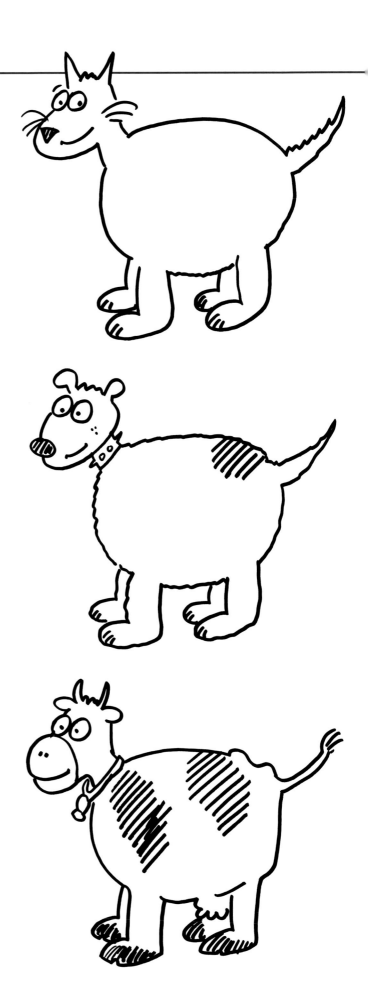

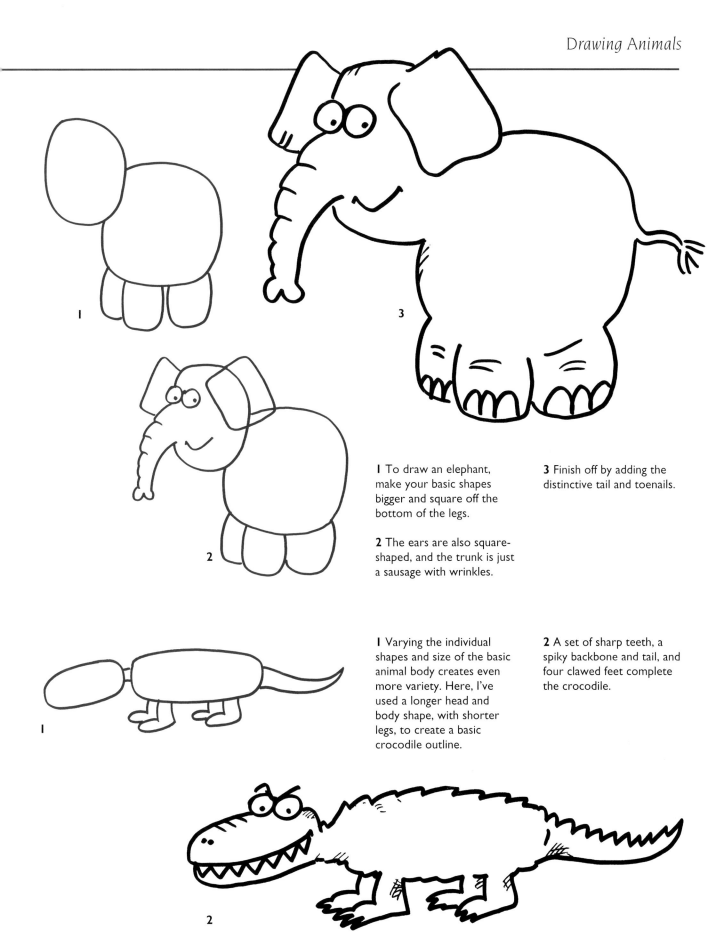

1 To draw an elephant, make your basic shapes bigger and square off the bottom of the legs.

2 The ears are also square-shaped, and the trunk is just a sausage with wrinkles.

3 Finish off by adding the distinctive tail and toenails.

1 Varying the individual shapes and size of the basic animal body creates even more variety. Here, I've used a longer head and body shape, with shorter legs, to create a basic crocodile outline.

2 A set of sharp teeth, a spiky backbone and tail, and four clawed feet complete the crocodile.

Proportion

It's good to know the rules of proportion – the sizes that different parts of the body should be in relation to each other. With cartoons, though, you don't always have to stick to these rules. Have fun experimenting with the sizes of your basic shapes. What happens if you make the head bigger, or the legs shorter? Can you make the figure look older by making all the shapes thinner and curving the body slightly? How much can you exaggerate your drawing and still keep the basic shape right?

Children and babies

You can play around with proportion in cartoons as much as you like, but there is one occasion when you do need to stick to the rules, and that is when drawing children and babies – an essential part of any cartoon cast.

One of the most common mistakes artists make is drawing children to look like small adults. You can see below that it's the *proportions* of the body, rather than the *size,* which hold the key.

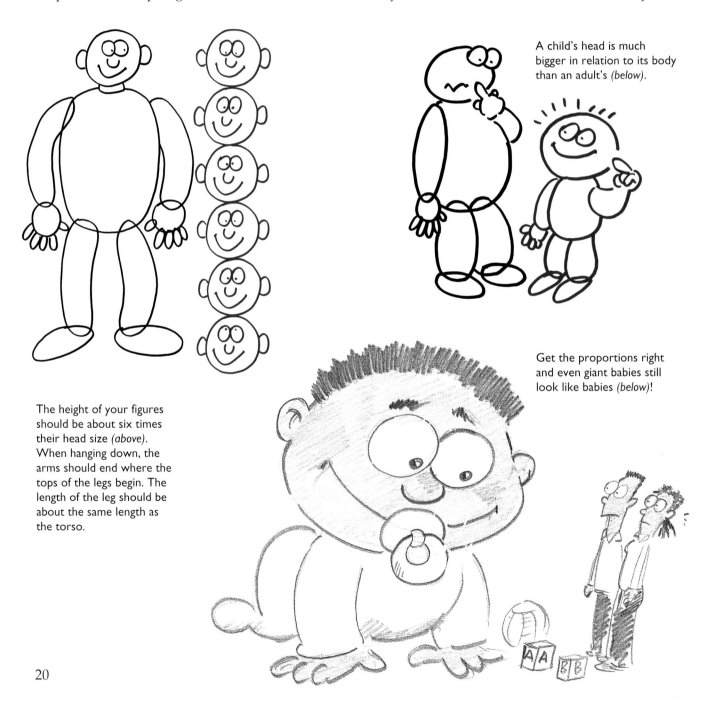

A child's head is much bigger in relation to its body than an adult's *(below)*.

The height of your figures should be about six times their head size *(above)*. When hanging down, the arms should end where the tops of the legs begin. The length of the leg should be about the same length as the torso.

Get the proportions right and even giant babies still look like babies *(below)*!

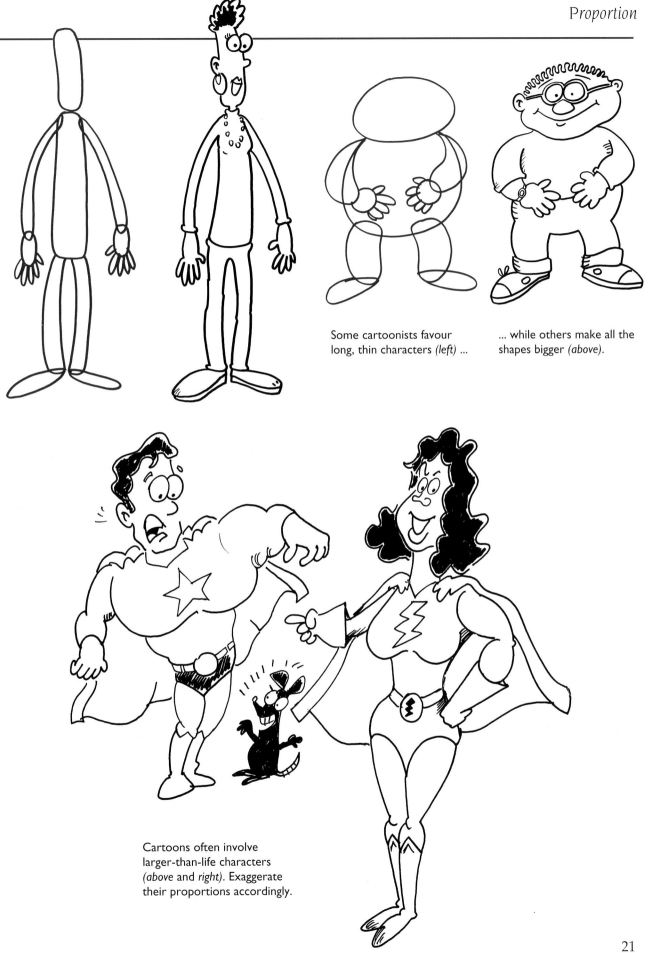

Some cartoonists favour long, thin characters *(left)* ...

... while others make all the shapes bigger *(above)*.

Cartoons often involve larger-than-life characters *(above* and *right)*. Exaggerate their proportions accordingly.

Character

Once you can draw the basic body shape, the next step is to try to create individual characters. The easiest way to do this is to add a wide selection of eyes, ears, noses and other physical features to your cartoon 'toolbox'. It's surprising how many different ways you can combine these features to give your cartoon characters distinctive personalities.

Eyes, ears and noses
Drawing eyes, ears and noses can also play an important part in developing your own cartoon style. A cartoonist may draw lots of very different characters but, by always drawing the eyes, nose or some other feature in the same way, the artist's work develops its own individual personality, instantly recognizable to fans and admirers everywhere.

Until you evolve your own style , try to vary the appearance of your characters' features. You can get ideas by observing the people around you, the faces you see in magazines or on television. Young, old, male, female, black, white, Asian ... everyone has their own unique combination of physical characteristics. Remember the features you find particularly interesting and try to add them to your own characters.

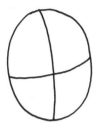

1 Start off with a basic head shape in pencil. The cross will help you keep all the bits and pieces in the right places, and in proportion.

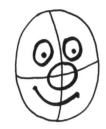

2 Now add simple eyes, ears, nose and mouth.

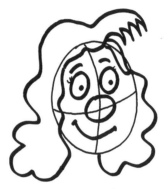

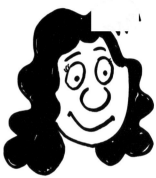

3 Finish off with eyebrows, lashes and a suitable hairstyle.

4 You can rub out the guidelines before drawing in your finished cartoon.

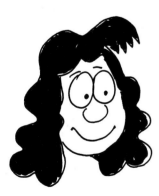

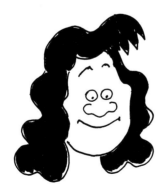

As we did with the basic body, the real fun starts when you change different parts of the cartoon face to create different characters (*above* and *right*). See what happens when you make the eyes bigger; the nose wider; or leave out certain features altogether. You can create even more variety by making the shape of the head wider or narrower.

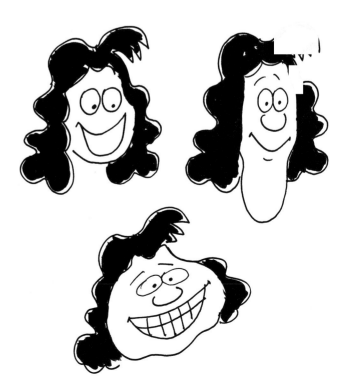

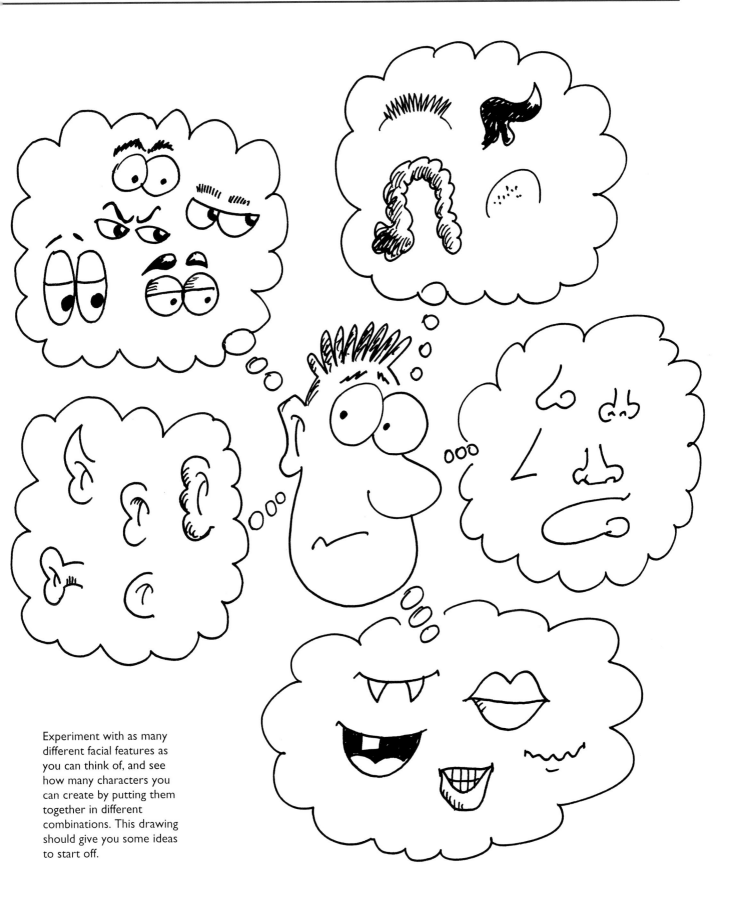

Experiment with as many different facial features as you can think of, and see how many characters you can create by putting them together in different combinations. This drawing should give you some ideas to start off.

Hands and feet

A person's hands can tell you a lot about them – a vampire's claws can tell you even more! As you can see below, changing the size or shape of a figure's hands and feet can change the whole character.

When giving your characters hands and feet, do try to give them different things to do with their right and left hands, and think about how they will stand on their feet. Always having both hands do the same thing can make your cartoon figures look very boring and symmetrical.

Age differences

Look closely at the differences between the hair, hands and feet of younger and older people. For instance, younger people, especially babies, tend to have short, fat fingers, while older hands may have longer, more wrinkled fingers.

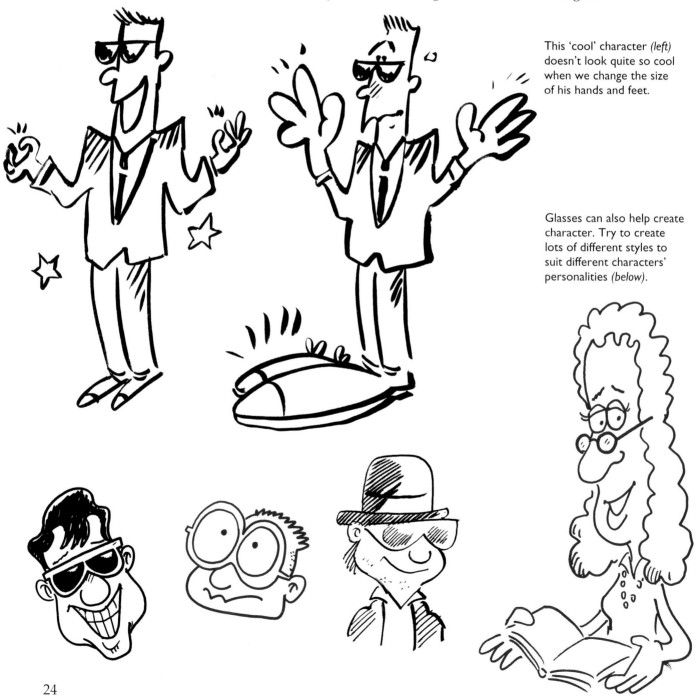

This 'cool' character *(left)* doesn't look quite so cool when we change the size of his hands and feet.

Glasses can also help create character. Try to create lots of different styles to suit different characters' personalities *(below)*.

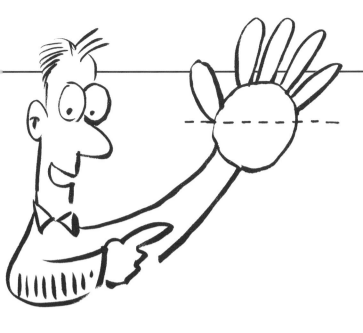

The basic hand shape is just a circle with the thumb starting about halfway down *(left)*.

Many cartoon characters have only three fingers – making it easier to move the hand around without getting the dreaded 'bunch-of-bananas' effect *(right)*.

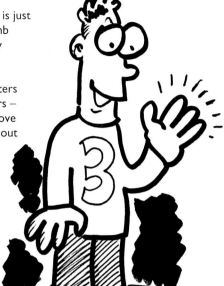

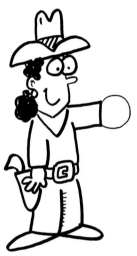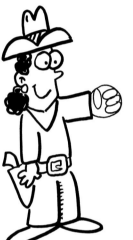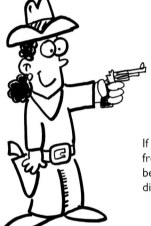

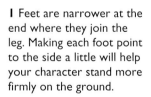

If you construct the hands from basic shapes, it should be easy to move them into different positions *(left)*.

1 Feet are narrower at the end where they join the leg. Making each foot point to the side a little will help your character stand more firmly on the ground.

2 The shape of the finished feet is squarer at the heel than in the rough drawing, and now there are only four toes on each foot – five can look a bit crowded. Don't forget to put in the big toenails.

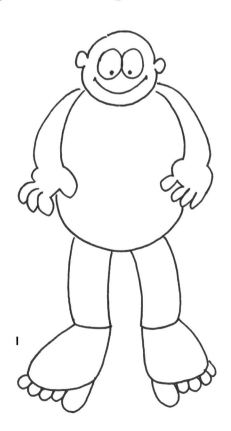

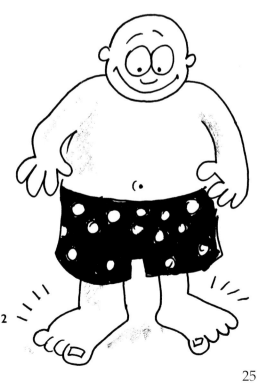

Expressions and Gestures

Once you've made your characters look interesting, now is the time to really bring them to life by providing them with a full range of facial expressions and gestures. You'll be surprised at how many different moods you can create just by making a few changes to your characters' features, movements and posture. Look in a mirror and see how many of your own expressions and gestures can be translated into cartoons.

Larger than life

Remember that cartoon characters have exaggerated emotions: when they are sad, they howl; when they are surprised, their eyes pop out of their heads; when they are angry, steam comes out of their ears. Sometimes all these things happen at once! Many cartoonists use a mirror to look at their own expressions, and then see just how far they can exaggerate them in cartoon form.

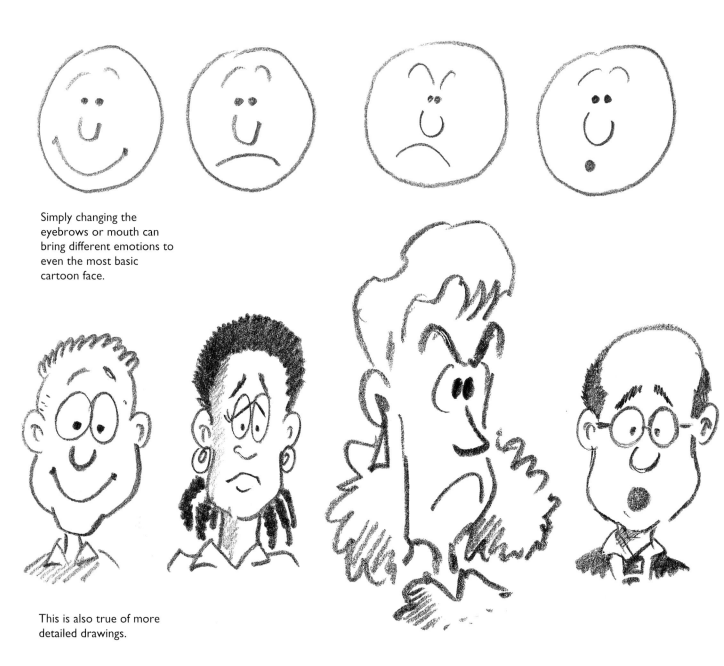

Simply changing the eyebrows or mouth can bring different emotions to even the most basic cartoon face.

This is also true of more detailed drawings.

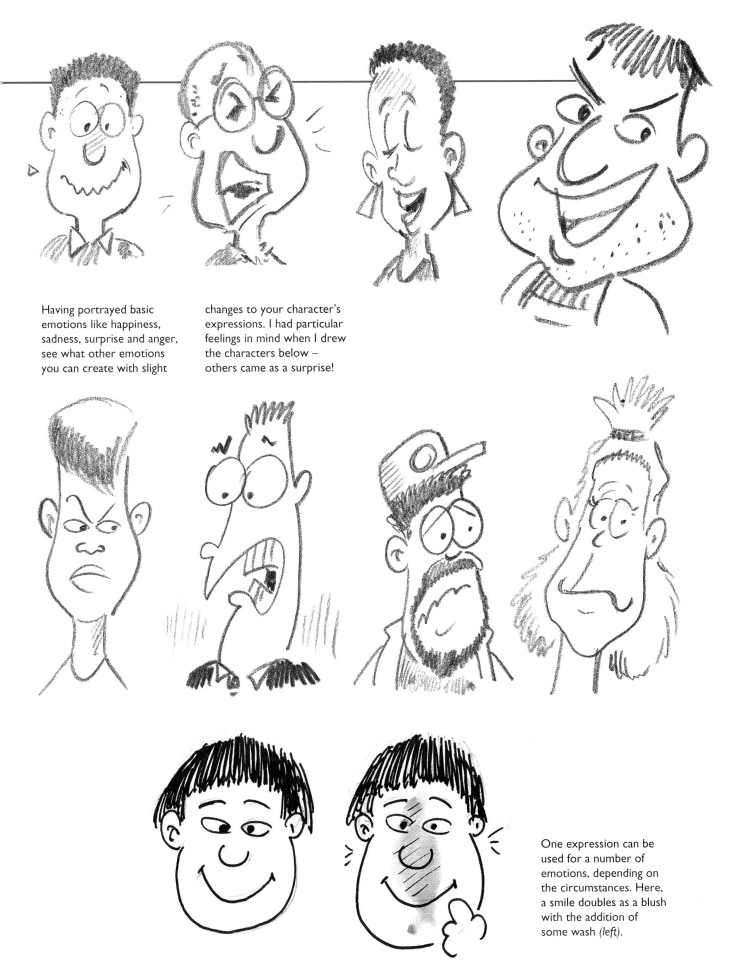

Having portrayed basic emotions like happiness, sadness, surprise and anger, see what other emotions you can create with slight changes to your character's expressions. I had particular feelings in mind when I drew the characters below – others came as a surprise!

One expression can be used for a number of emotions, depending on the circumstances. Here, a smile doubles as a blush with the addition of some wash *(left)*.

Silent language

As well as watching yourself in the mirror, another excellent way of studying the way people express their feelings is to watch television with the sound turned down. Can you work out what people are saying, and how they are feeling, from their gestures and facial expressions? Your cartoon characters should be able to communicate in the same way.

Creating the mood

When you are showing your character's feelings, choose a drawing medium and colours that will help set the mood. Soft pencils and bright colours can be used to create the impression of peace and happiness, a scratchy pen, giving a jagged line, can make an angry character look even fiercer, while lots of grey tones can be used for a sad picture.

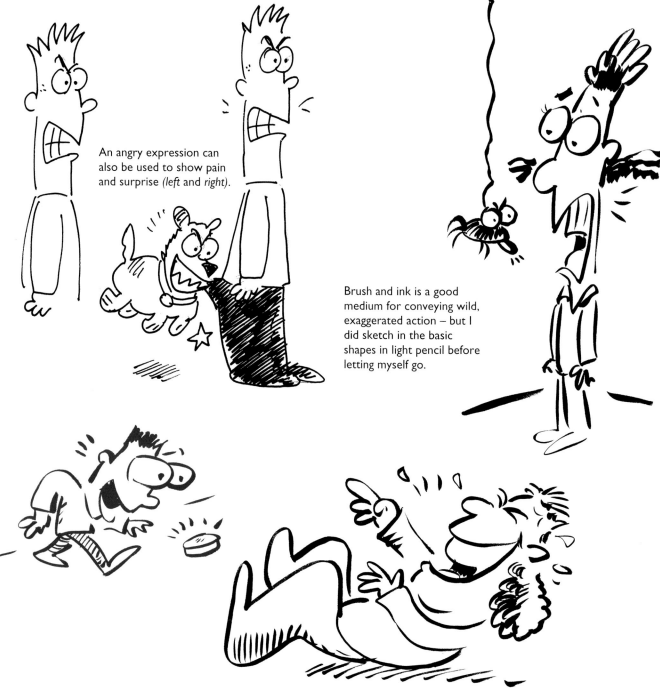

An angry expression can also be used to show pain and surprise (*left* and *right*).

Brush and ink is a good medium for conveying wild, exaggerated action – but I did sketch in the basic shapes in light pencil before letting myself go.

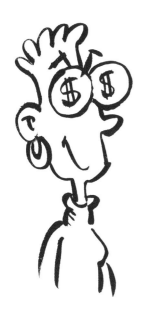 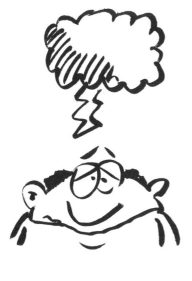 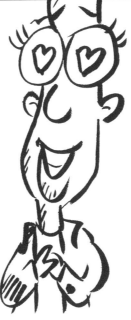 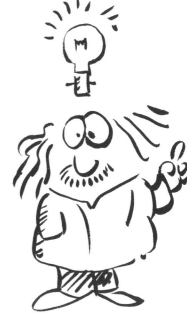

While you can make your cartoon characters run through a whole range of emotions by altering eyes, mouths and eyebrows, cartoonists have also

evolved a language of symbols which you can add to your drawings to emphasize feelings even more. Here are: Greed ($ or £ signs in eyes);

Gloom (under a cloud); Love (hearts in eyes); and Inspiration (light bulb lights up above head). Can you invent some symbols of your own?

If these figures could speak, this might be what they were saying:

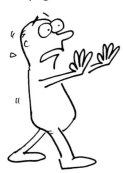 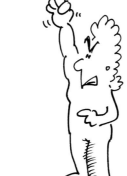 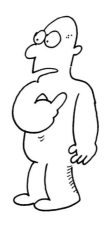

'Please don't hit me!'

'I'll get you for this!'

'Who? Me?'

'How should I know?'

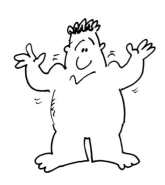 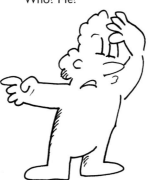

'I want to be alone!'

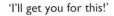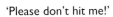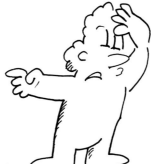

Artist's Tip

The same gesture can mean different things to different people ... it's best to check first to avoid giving offence!

29

Clothing and Props

Do you have a favourite suit? A pair of jeans you've worn long past their throwing-away date? A hat that all your friends instantly recognize as belonging to you? Your choice of clothes can reveal a lot about your personality, and the same goes for your cartoon characters.

The language of clothes

Cartoonists often rely on instantly recognizable uniforms to denote a character's nationality or profession. Clothes can also place characters in a certain period of history – although some continue to wear distinctive uniforms long after they are out-of-date. Getting the message across matters more than historical accuracy.

Neat or sloppy?

Adding clothes to the basic figure shape isn't difficult, but do look closely at how they 'hang' on people's bodies. How we wear our clothes says as much about us as the styles we choose.

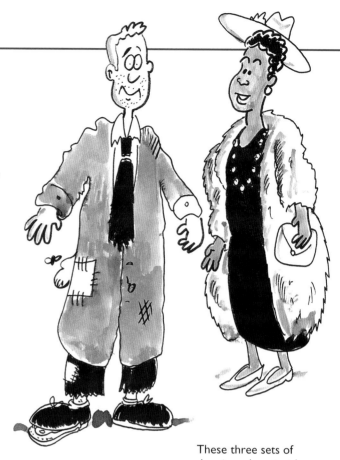

These three sets of drawings show just how dramatically different clothes can change the identity of the same cartoon character.

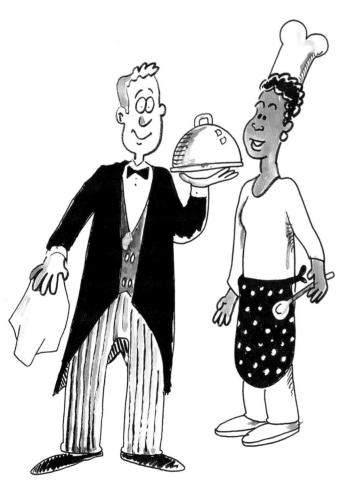

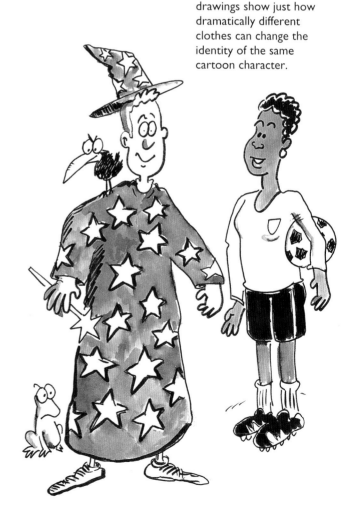

Fashion up-date

Try to keep up-to-date on fashions for men, women, and on the way young people dress. If you still draw people in clothes that were out-of-date 20 years ago, your cartoons may get laughed at for all the wrong reasons!

Keep an eye out for fashion articles and photos in newspapers and magazines. As well as showing you lots of different clothes to draw, they are also good for practice in cartooning the human figure. Supermodels will look even more super after you've given them the cartoon treatment!

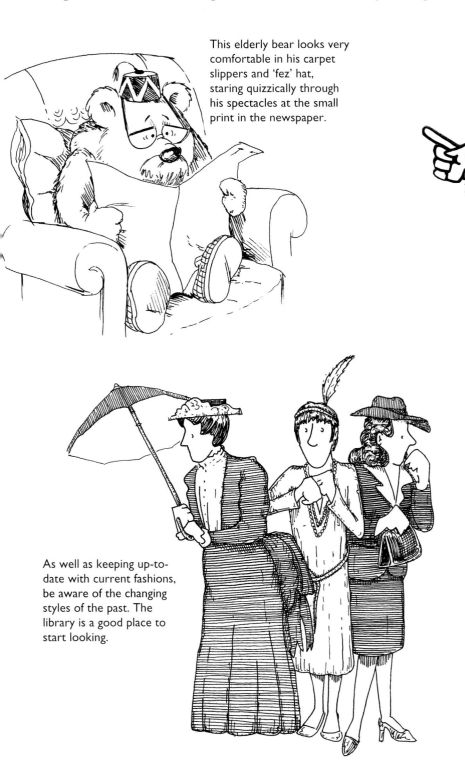

This elderly bear looks very comfortable in his carpet slippers and 'fez' hat, staring quizzically through his spectacles at the small print in the newspaper.

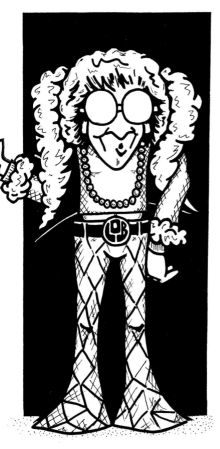

You can have fun drawing way-out fashions, such as the 'cool dude' in the cartoon above. But beware. Getting the current fashions wrong could start people laughing *at* your cartoons, instead of along with them.

As well as keeping up-to-date with current fashions, be aware of the changing styles of the past. The library is a good place to start looking.

Props

'Props' are another important tool for telling us all about a character's position in life. As with costume, many cartoon characters continue using the same props long after their real-life counterparts have stopped – like the pipe and magnifying glass of the Sherlock Holmes lookalike below.

Getting the props to look right can add a great deal to a cartoon's authenticity. Many cartoonists keep large supplies of old magazines as reference material, but if you're short on living space, a good library should fulfil the task just as well.

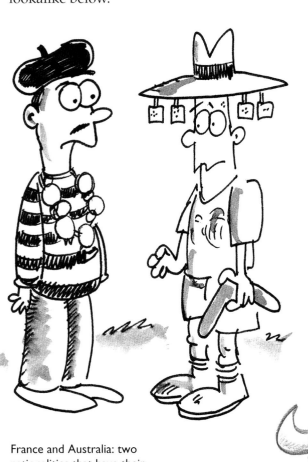

Most teachers don't dress like this anymore *(right)*, but it's a cartoon image that seems to live on forever.

France and Australia: two nationalities that have their 'standard' cartoon costume *(above)*. How many others can you think of?

'It's for you.'

Period costume like the vikings' distinctive helmets are good for creating joke ideas *(right)*.

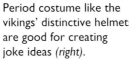

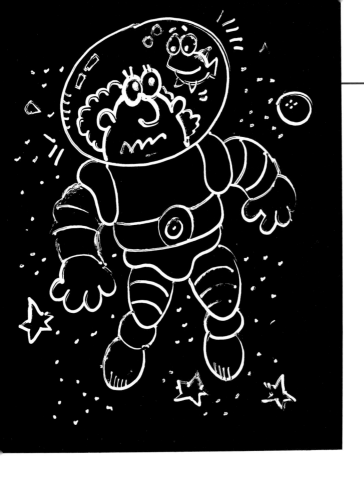

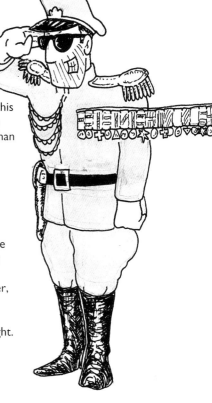

Futuristic costumes like this spacesuit *(left)* often owe more to science fiction than the real thing.

Note how many small details have gone to make up this authentic-looking military costume *(right)*. Besides the boots, holster, braids and medals, the shape of the hat and trousers must also be right.

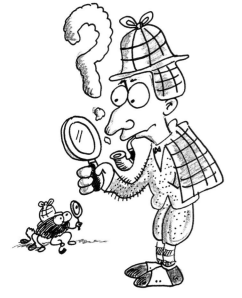

Where would the cartoon detective be without pipe and magnifying glass *(above)*?

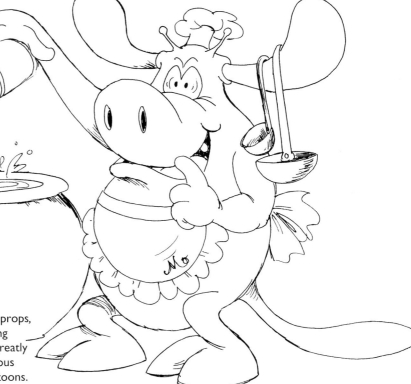

Getting the correct props, such as these cooking utensils *(right)*, can greatly increase the humorous content of your cartoons.

Turning Animals into People

One of the most common cartoon techniques is 'anthropomorphism' – a big word that simply means giving animals and objects human characteristics. Many animated cartoon stars are humanized animals and you should have no problem combining the drawing skills you've already learned to create your own characters.

Choosing your subject

As with drawing cartoon people, your humanized animals will look a lot more realistic if you spend some time studying their real-life counterparts. Have your sketchbook ready next time you visit a wildlife park or even when you are watching nature programmes on TV. Don't just stick to the usual cartoon menagerie of dogs, cats, mice, etc. You've got the whole insect, bird and undersea world to explore, too. Do a little research and you'll be amazed at the variety of creatures that live with us on the planet – some are even stranger than anything a cartoonist might think of!

But just as it's important to give your human characters individual personalities, you'll need to make your cartoon creatures distinctive, too. Remember that many funny cartoon characters are created by giving a particular animal or object a personality that's completely different from the one we would normally associate with it. For instance, you could make a lion cowardly instead of brave, or turn a fluffy rabbit into a bad-tempered bully.

Altering an animal's usual size and proportions can increase the comic effect still further – enlarging that rabbit to giant size will make it look much fiercer and more threatening.

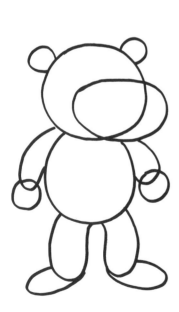

1 I've pencilled in my basic human shape again, but added a lion's head. As I've chosen quite a big animal, I've made my basic shapes big and fat.

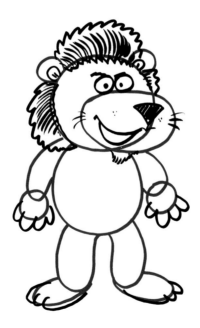

2 Even though I'm doing a cartoon lion, I've tried to keep some realistic features, such as the tuft of hair under the chin.

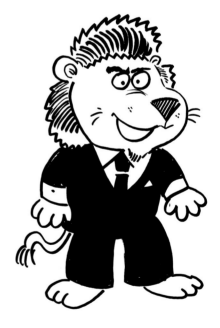

3 Finally, a smart suit for the king of beasts ... but I haven't forgotten to leave room at the back for a tail.

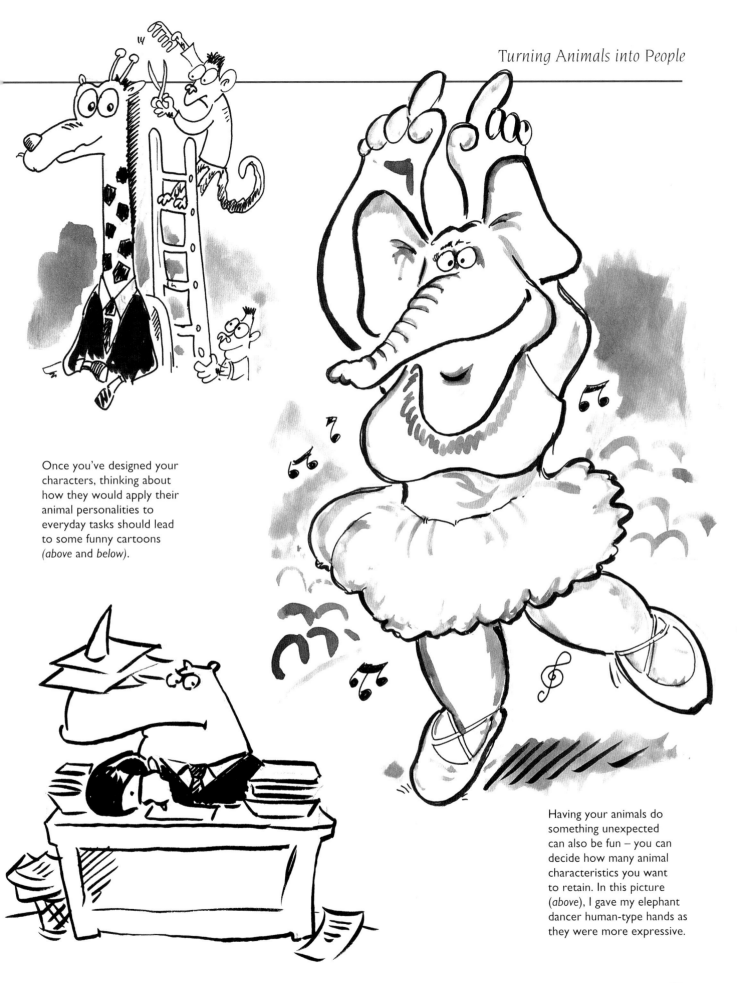

Once you've designed your characters, thinking about how they would apply their animal personalities to everyday tasks should lead to some funny cartoons (*above* and *below*).

Having your animals do something unexpected can also be fun – you can decide how many animal characteristics you want to retain. In this picture (*above*), I gave my elephant dancer human-type hands as they were more expressive.

Living objects

Just as you can turn animals into personalities you can also use your cartoon skills to bring inanimate objects to life, again giving them appropriate characteristics. As with animals, you'll find that objects look most effective if you try to sketch the real thing first and identify its unique features.

When you add features to your cartoon objects, think about the kind of personality or expression you want them to have. For example, if you have drawn a big, powerful-looking limousine, why not make it very nervous about speeding?

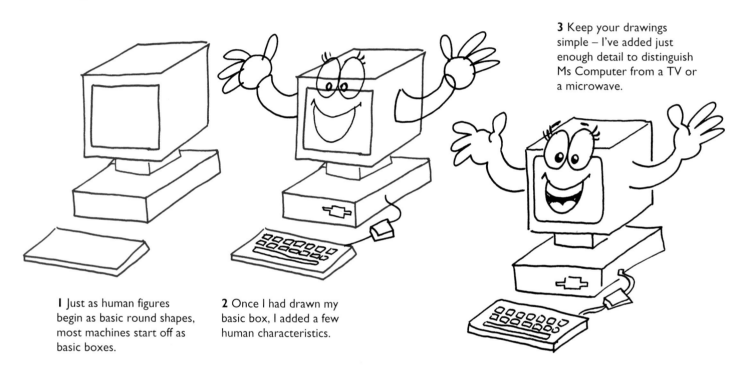

3 Keep your drawings simple – I've added just enough detail to distinguish Ms Computer from a TV or a microwave.

1 Just as human figures begin as basic round shapes, most machines start off as basic boxes.

2 Once I had drawn my basic box, I added a few human characteristics.

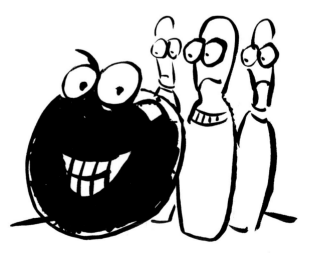

With the addition of cartoon eyes, almost anything can be brought to life (*left*).

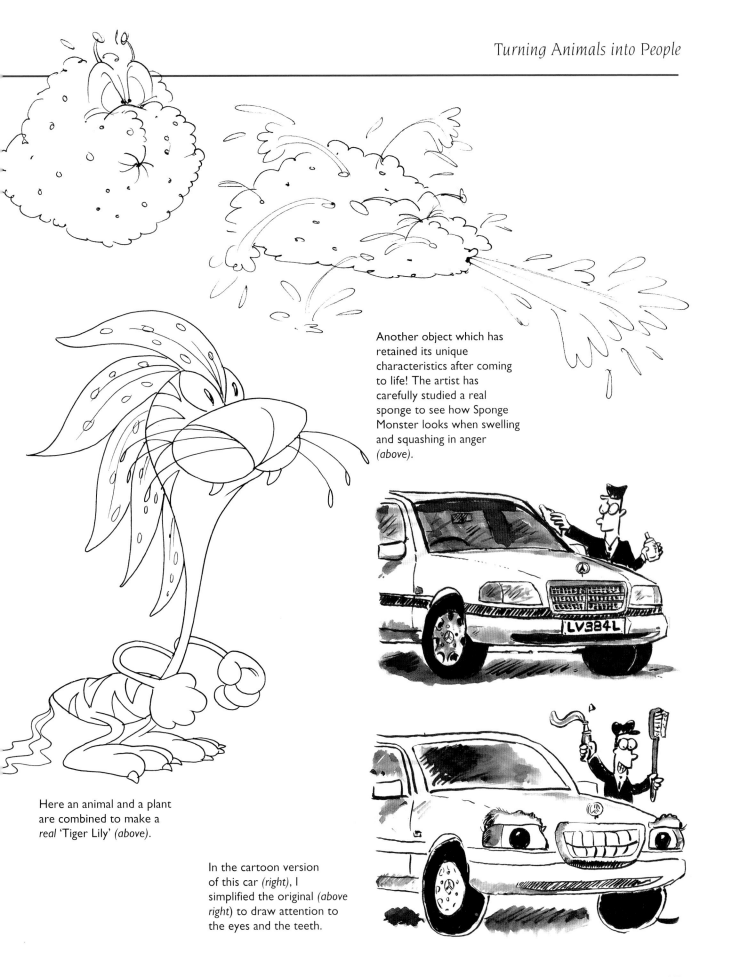

Another object which has retained its unique characteristics after coming to life! The artist has carefully studied a real sponge to see how Sponge Monster looks when swelling and squashing in anger *(above)*.

Here an animal and a plant are combined to make a *real* 'Tiger Lily' *(above)*.

In the cartoon version of this car *(right)*, I simplified the original *(above right)* to draw attention to the eyes and the teeth.

LV384L

Perspective

All artists need to know about perspective. In fact, whole books have been written on this important subject. Luckily you'll only need to learn a little about perspective to make a big difference to the success of your cartoons.

Knowing about perspective will not only make your cartoons look more 'real' (even the crazy ones!) but will help you add depth to your cartoon world.

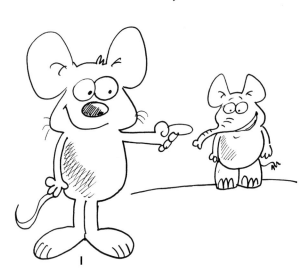

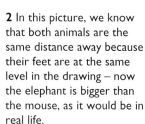

2

1 The near-and-far rule applies whenever you are drawing a character or object in perspective: parts that are nearest will be bigger than parts that are further away – as you can see from this giant mouse and tiny elephant.

2 In this picture, we know that both animals are the same distance away because their feet are at the same level in the drawing – now the elephant is bigger than the mouse, as it would be in real life.

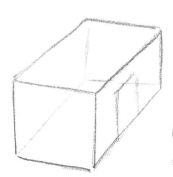

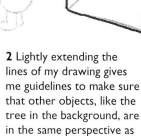

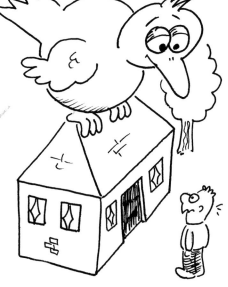

1 I start all of my buildings as simple block shapes. The shape of each side slants inwards as it gets further away. As we are looking from above, we can also see the top of the shape.

2 Lightly extending the lines of my drawing gives me guidelines to make sure that other objects, like the tree in the background, are in the same perspective as the house.

3 To give an idea of scale, we need to put something of known size in the cartoon for comparison. In my finished drawing, the normal-sized person, house and tree emphasize the fact

that someone has been overfeeding the canary on the roof!

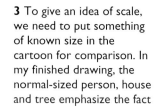

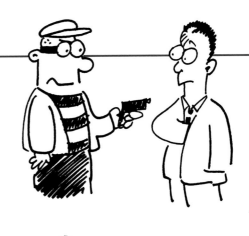

I've explained the basic rules of perspective below. With a little practice you'll soon be able to try out further experiments for yourself.

Adding distance

A simple way of showing how far or near objects in your cartoons are is to remember that the further away an object is, the smaller it will be on your page. Faraway objects will also be higher up on the page.

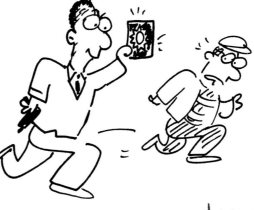

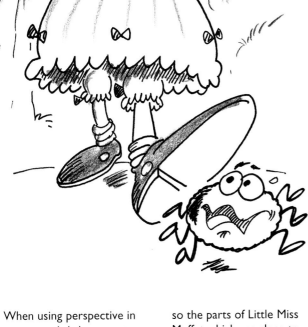

Objects tend to become lighter as they recede into the distance. The black areas on the robber's clothes in the first picture (top) become lighter cross hatched areas as he tries to escape (above), making him look further away.

When using perspective in a cartoon, it is important to decide which eye level we will view the picture from. In this picture, our eye level is the same as the spider's on the ground, so the parts of Little Miss Muffet which are close to us are drawn much bigger, while her head and shoulders are smaller and further away. This trick is called 'foreshortening'.

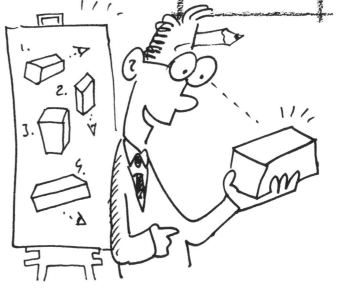

Movement and Action

Once you start moving your cartoon characters around, you'll see the big advantage of building them up from basic shapes. As well as making even the most complicated movements easy to draw, basing your characters on the same simple shapes will make them recognizable as the same individuals, no matter how many different poses you draw them in.

Strike a pose

If you can find a full-length mirror, you can strike some poses yourself and see what happens to the different parts of your body every time you move. You may even be able to persuade a friend to model for you – after all, who would turn down a cartoon original as a reward?

If you study your own movements carefully, or those of your 'model', you will notice that it isn't just the arms that change position with each new pose – the whole body is involved. Does the body lean forward or backward slightly? Does the head drop down or stretch upwards?

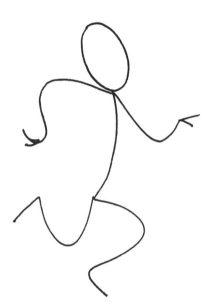

1 I usually start a movement drawing by trying lots of different matchstick figures until I draw one that best suits the pose I want.

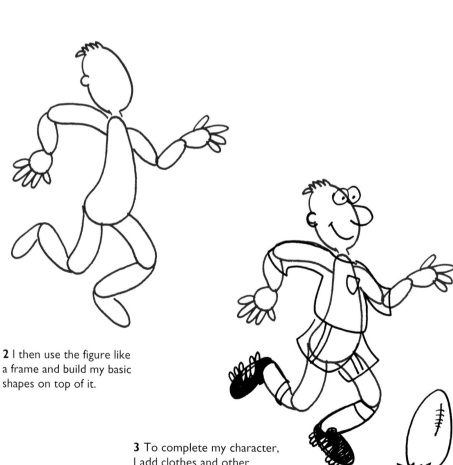

2 I then use the figure like a frame and build my basic shapes on top of it.

3 To complete my character, I add clothes and other details to the figure.

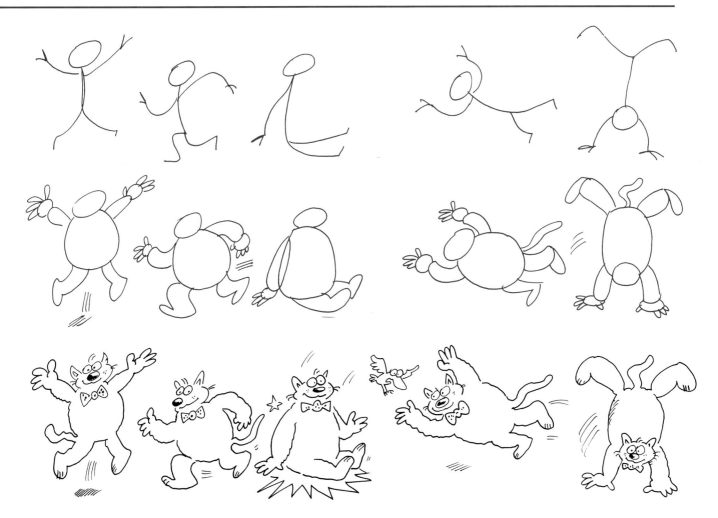

Try making one of your cartoon characters perform as many different movements as you can

think of (above). If you have used simple shapes to build your character, you will find that you can draw it in

any position you like and it will always look the same. This is particularly useful in story sequences, as in the

comic strips on pages 52-55 and simple animation on page 63.

In the first drawing (right), this character appears to be jogging slowly. Lifting him off the ground and adding a puff of steam, a bead of sweat, and some movement lines (far right) makes him appear to run much faster. Notice that his body pose hasn't changed at all.

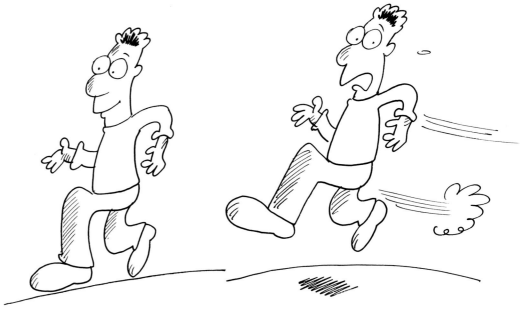

Larger than life

Exaggeration is an important part of cartoon action – our heroes and heroines don't always do things like real people – they run faster, hit harder and jump higher. See how far you can stretch each movement, but don't overdo it: remember each action still has to be recognizable for the cartoon to work.

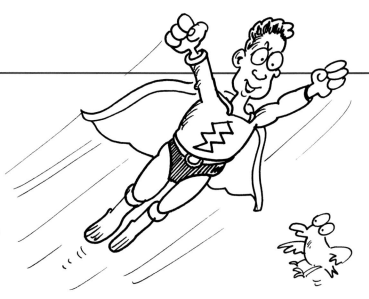

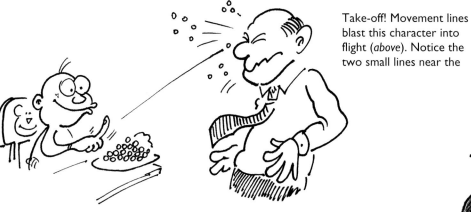

Take-off! Movement lines blast this character into flight (*above*). Notice the two small lines near the

bird's feet which tell us that she has literally stopped in mid-air, in her surprise at this flying figure.

The movement line helps us follow the path of the peas. Here it is the expression on

the victim's face that shows us that they have hit their target (*above*).

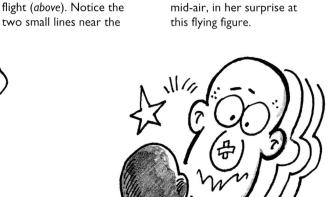

Two cartoonist's symbols: the repeated lines around the head create a vibration effect, while the stars exaggerate the impact of the glove (*above*).

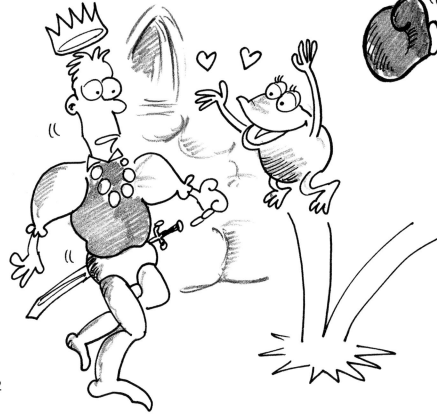

Here (*left*), movement lines are combined with a star shape to create a frog who can really BOUNCE!

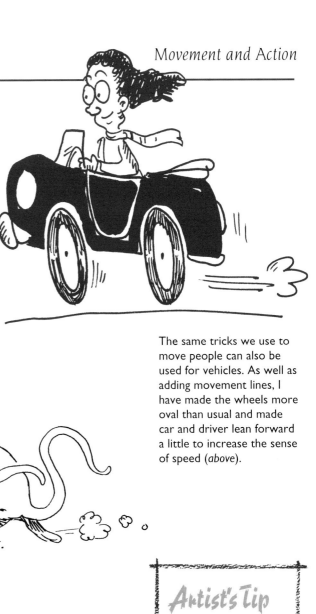

Using symbols

To make life easier, cartoonists have a whole range of symbols and tricks to indicate and exaggerate motion, such as the movement lines around the figure of the musician. Practise using them in your drawings ... or invent your own.

These mice are leaning forward while running *(below)* which makes them appear to move all the faster.

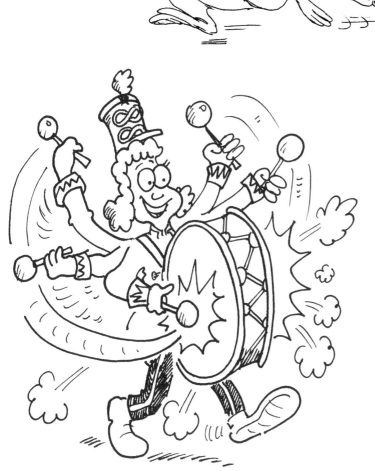

The same tricks we use to move people can also be used for vehicles. As well as adding movement lines, I have made the wheels more oval than usual and made car and driver lean forward a little to increase the sense of speed *(above)*.

Drawing multiple arms or legs in the same cartoon is another way to give the effect of very fast movement. In this drawing *(left)*, movement and impact symbols give the impression of deafening sound and frantic action.

Artist's Tip

When you draw your movement lines, make sure they don't actually touch your cartoon characters, or you'll hold them back instead of helping them go faster.

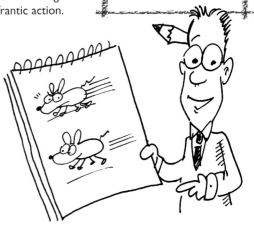

43

Backgrounds and Scenery

Once you've created a cast of cartoon characters, you need a world for them to live in. Cartoon backgrounds can be simple or complicated, but the main thing to bear in mind is that they must never distract from the main 'actors' in your drawings. That's why so many cartoons and comic strips have little or no background detail. However, the right setting can be a big help in creating atmosphere in your cartoons and jokes.

Selecting the detail
On these pages you'll see how one or two carefully chosen details can stand in for a complete scene, a city – or even a country. The trick is to choose the right details to give the impression of a particular scene or background.

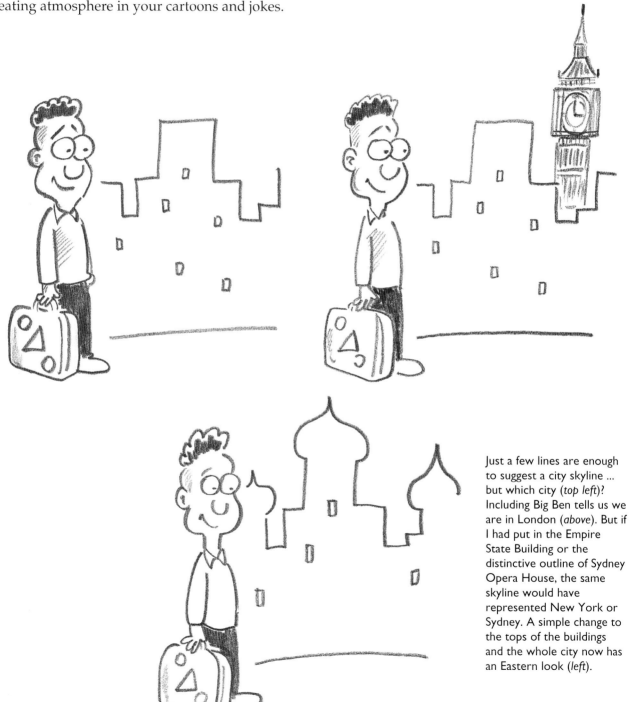

Just a few lines are enough to suggest a city skyline ... but which city (*top left*)? Including Big Ben tells us we are in London (*above*). But if I had put in the Empire State Building or the distinctive outline of Sydney Opera House, the same skyline would have represented New York or Sydney. A simple change to the tops of the buildings and the whole city now has an Eastern look (*left*).

Real-life backgrounds

Look around you as you read this book. Whether you are indoors or outdoors, most rooms, streets and even areas of countryside look basically the same. It's the details that make the difference. For instance, you will usually find a filing cabinet in an office rather than a living room. The main street of a city has the big stores and restaurants – you are more likely to find smaller, more unusual shops in the back streets. The plants and trees that grow in the desert will be very different from the ones that grow in the Arctic.

When you are drawing such scenes, it helps to find pictures of the details you want so that you can copy them.

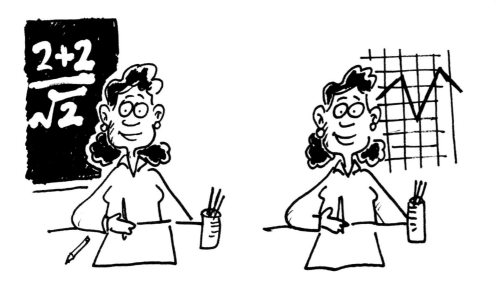

The same woman sitting behind the same desk – but the blackboard in the first drawing *(far left)* suggests a classroom scene. Replacing it with a graph in the second drawing *(left)* moves the cartoon to an office setting.

Different background details can tell us just as much about cartoon characters as their costumes can. The windows in these pictures are in very different types of home – and tell us a lot about the income of the person who lives there *(below left* and *below right)*.

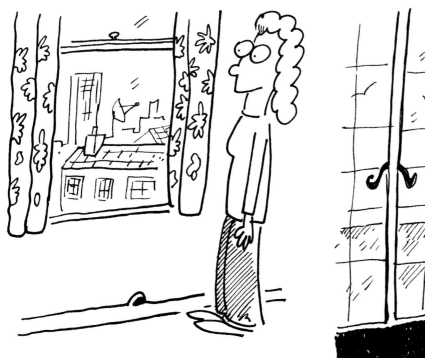

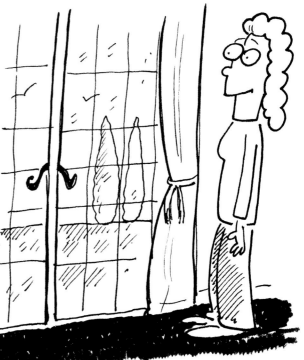

Giveaway clues

Sometimes a single detail is enough to tell us exactly where the scene is taking place. A famous building or some other landmark can turn a standard drawing of a city into a particular city (see page 44). My wife might say that a messy desk is a big clue that an office scene is taking place in my office! Looking around you right now, is there one particular piece of furniture, building or other object you would pick to represent the whole scene? Add it to a cartoon and see if people can locate the setting.

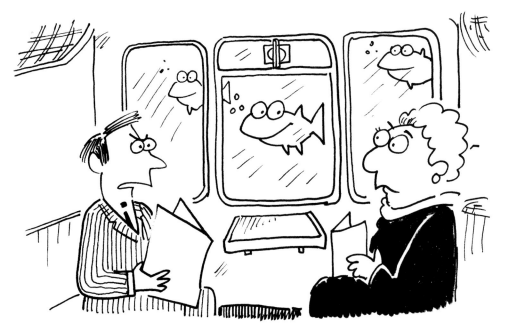

Here's a cartoon where the background is part of the joke *(left)*. It was important to make the train inside look quite realistic, to make the fish seem all the more out of place. The caption might read:
'I wish you'd stop asking if this is the right train.'

Crowds are useful for all kinds of background. Look closely at this cartoon *(right)* and you'll see that you only need to draw a couple of people at the front in any great detail. Lots and lots of head shapes do the rest.

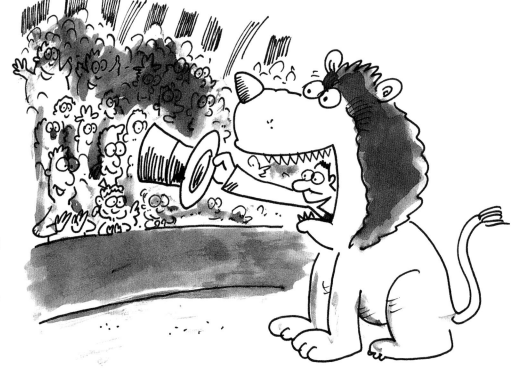

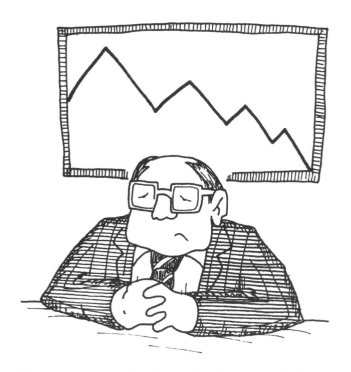

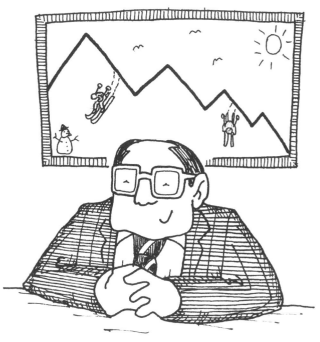

Here is another example of a cartoon in which the joke is in the background detail, not in the figure (*above*).

Note that, except for the eyes and mouth, the drawing of the businessman doesn't change at all.

Mechanical tone is useful when you set your cartoons somewhere dark, but still need to show the background details (*right*).

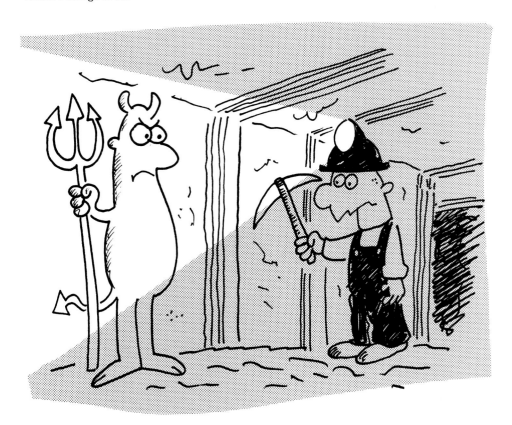

Caricature

Caricature is one of the most popular cartooning skills, but can be very daunting for beginners. It's true that the more your cartooning skills improve, the greater the likeness you will be able to convey. Just like other forms of cartooning, however, caricature involves working with basic shapes.

Starting with the basics
Try to identify the basic shapes that make up your subject's face and start building up your sketch from this foundation. In the beginning, you may find it easier to work from a photograph rather than a real-life model so that you can spend as long as you need to get a good likeness. Don't forget that even drawings by famous cartoonists, which seem to catch the likeness of a person with only a few brush and pen strokes, may well have taken many attempts to get right.

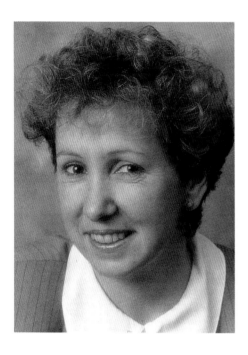

A friend lent me this photograph to caricature. She may live to regret it, but here goes ...

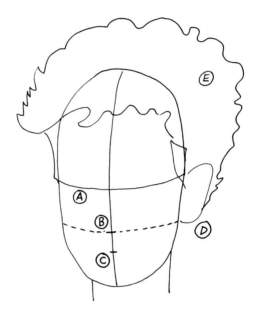

1 I began by drawing the basic face shape in pencil. Then I added guidelines to help me position the features in the right place. Line A, halfway down the face, is where I will put the eyes, while lines B and C mark the nose and mouth. Even though I am doing a caricature I have tried to keep these features the same distance apart as in the photo. I also know that lines A and B mark the top and bottom of the ear shape (D). Finally I drew the hair shape (E).

2 Now I can start identifying the individual details which give the face its personality. The eyes are always important, and I've tried hard to capture the exact shape. Don't be afraid to use your eraser and keep trying until you get it right. I've made the mouth a bit bigger than in real life but I've still tried to keep the shape. Note that I've altered my basic face outline to keep the distance between the larger mouth and tip of the chin the same as in the photo.

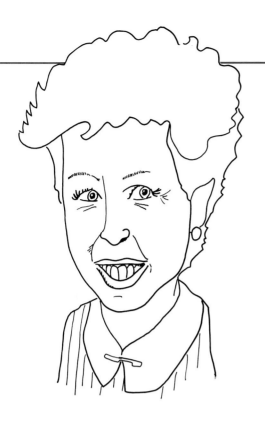

Special features
Once you've established some basic outlines, look for the most striking aspects of your subject's appearance and then exaggerate them. (If the subject is someone you work or live with, you may find it wise to check that they share your sense of humour before showing them the result!). Another way to highlight a feature is to leave almost every other feature out of your drawing.

3 It's time for a bit of exaggeration. I've made the eyelashes longer, the teeth bigger, and the lines around the eyes more definite. I've also made the earring a bit bigger, but not too much – I didn't want to lose the shape of the ear.

4 The face is only part of a caricature. Putting as many other clues as possible in the picture will help you get a likeness. This person works in a busy office so I finished off by giving her a crowded desk, phone and filing cabinet.

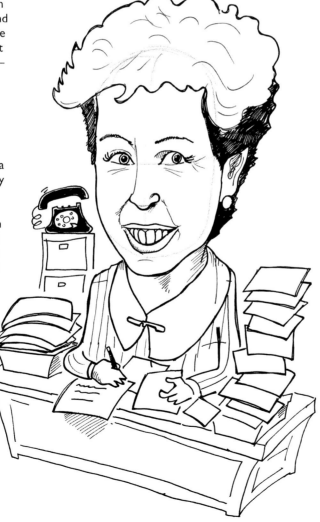

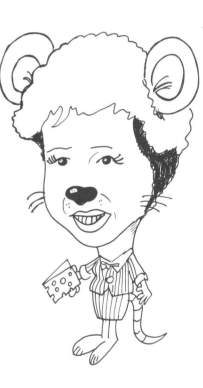

Once you've identified a person's unique characteristics, you can draw them as an object or animal and still keep them recognizable.

Famous faces

If the person you are drawing is famous, try to find some caricatures of them done by professional cartoonists. Don't just try to copy what has been done before, but observe which details of the person's face the cartoonist has chosen to exaggerate. (You may well find that two different cartoonists have come up with very different ways of drawing the same person.)

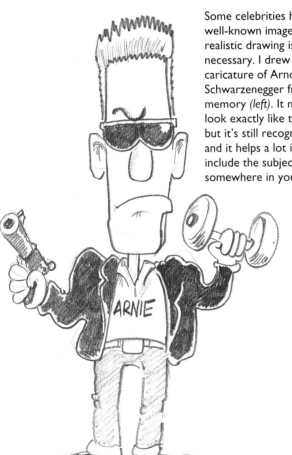

Some celebrities have such well-known images that a realistic drawing isn't necessary. I drew this caricature of Arnold Schwarzenegger from memory *(left)*. It may not look exactly like the actor but it's still recognizable ... and it helps a lot if you include the subject's name somewhere in your drawing!

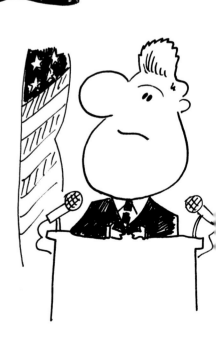

President Mandela *(right)* is almost a straight drawing, but the small body gives it more of a cartoon look.

President Clinton *(right)* has been caricatured so many thousands of times that it's possible to leave out almost everything except the distinctive nose and hairstyle. You can make caricatures of politicians easier to recognize by including some special symbol or prop – like the flag in this drawing, and in the drawing of President Mandela *(above)*.

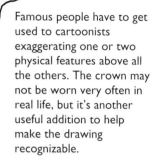

Clothing clues

We have already looked at how clothes and props can be an important part of a cartoon's character. The same is true of a caricature. For instance, a suitable prop such as a bat or ball or a musical instrument can make a big difference in identifying a particular sports or music star.

Famous people have to get used to cartoonists exaggerating one or two physical features above all the others. The crown may not be worn very often in real life, but it's another useful addition to help make the drawing recognizable.

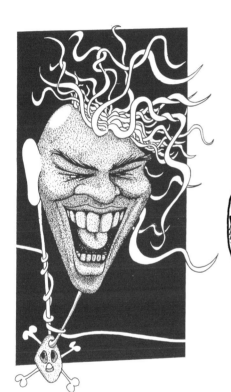

It takes some time to build up all these small dots of ink into a 'stipple' effect *(above)* but the finished result can make caricatures and facial expressions look all the more striking.

It's not just Mr Spock's distinctive ears and eyebrows that make this caricature work *(right)*: the facial expression is important, too. The shading on the costume helps to emphasize the stark black and white look of the face.

Artist's Tip

Drawing a real person can be scary! You can be so concerned about getting a likeness that you may find it hard to concentrate on identifying the basic shapes. Turning the picture you are copying upside-down will help switch your concentration from the 'personality' to the abstract shapes.

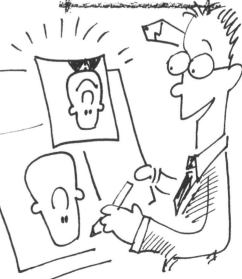

Comic Strips

Comic strips give you the chance really to try out your cartooning skills. You can practise all the things you have learned so far in the different panels of your strip.

Telling a story

Comic strips are not just a number of cartoons put together at random, however: you need to arrange your drawings in a sequence that tells a story. The story can use words or just pictures. It can feature just one character or several. It can be just a couple of panels long or take up a whole comic book. Whatever form your story takes, the important thing is to plan your sequence carefully to tell your story as simply and clearly as possible.

How to begin

Some cartoonists start off by designing their characters first, and then create a story around them. Thinking about how the different characters would cope with a particular situation can lead to lots of stories. For instance, the cowardly lion and brave mouse below would each behave in very different way if they were to stay in a haunted house.

Another way to do comic strips is to think up a funny story first and then invent characters to act it out. If you can't think of an original story, don't worry – many comics and cartoons start off as funny variations on well-known stories.

Here is a very simple story using just two panels which you could expand into a longer sequence *(below)*. What else could happen to these characters? How do they end up in the house in the first place? Will they escape or will they be trapped forever? Organize your ideas into a beginning, middle and end and you've got your story.

Artist's Tip

Most comic strips are drawn about TWICE the size of the pictures you see on the printed page. You'll find it much easier to draw your comic strips at the bigger size and reduce them on a photocopier at your local library, stationery shop or printer. Here is the first panel of the strip opposite at its original size for you to compare with the printed version.

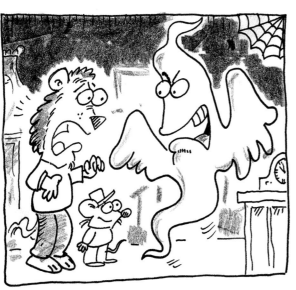

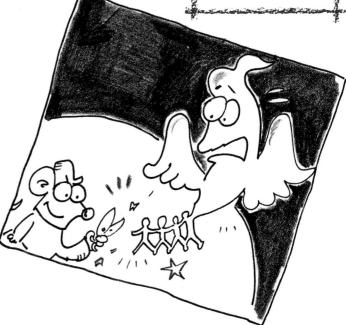

52

The superhero is a standard character in comic strips. Even though I'm going to play this story for laughs *(right)*, the same techniques can be used to tell a 'serious' adventure story.

1 I put quite a lot of detail into this picture to set the scene. I can then use little or no background in the remaining pictures. Notice how the picture in the 'thought balloon' starts the action.

2 I have moved in closer for a better look at what's going on in the window.

3 I've used a silhouette effect in this picture – making sure that my outlines are distinct enough so that the action is clear.

4 Changing the design of the box helps highlight dramatic moments.

5 You don't have to make all your panels the same size. A 'long shot' gives a full picture of the action. If you need extra space you can leave out some or all of the box as I have done here.

6 POW! Another way to highlight an exciting scene is to have parts of the drawing, such as the crook's hat and gun, break out of the box.

7 & 8 Meanwhile back at the restaurant ... I drew as little as possible of the diners in the last panel to emphasize the joke (yes, I know it's an old joke!). Why not try your own version of the story, and finish with a different surprise ending?

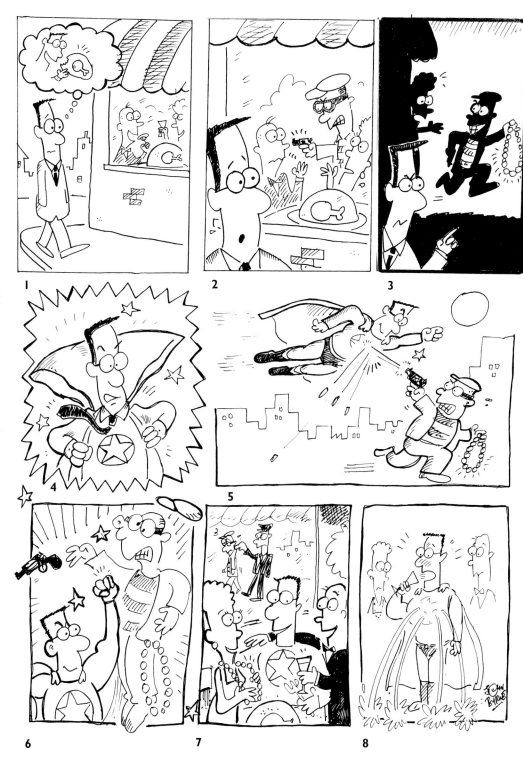

Thinking in pictures

Remember that cartoons and comics are supposed to be a visual medium. You'll be surprised at how many jokes sound very funny but don't work as comic strips. You can see from my rough sketches that I 'write' my stories as pictures so that I can think about how they will look as well as what's going to happen. I usually draw each sketch on a separate sheet of paper so that I can take out, add and even swap drawings around to tell the story better.

Producing finished artwork

Now that I have my story in rough form, it's much easier to plan my finished artwork. I know from my rough drawings how much space I need to leave on the page for each panel. If there isn't enough space, I may have to cut the number of drawings or combine two ideas in one picture.

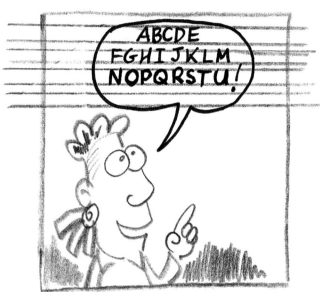

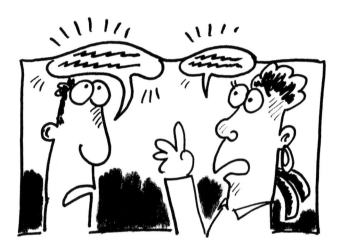

Don't forget to leave enough room in your panels for speech balloons. You may find it a bit of a squeeze to put them in after you've drawn the

picture *(above)*. I prefer to put in the balloons first while the drawing is still in pencil. The letter guidelines can be erased after ink has been added *(above right)*.

The action in this comic strip is self-explanatory, and so does not need speech bubbles *(below)*. I call this type of sequence a 'what happens next' strip.

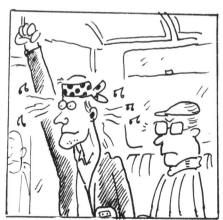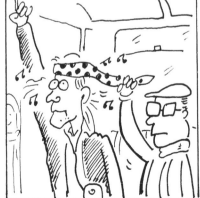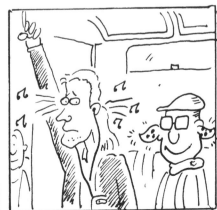

Looking at my finished strip, you'll see the main idea is to try to get as much variety into your individual panels as possible. I like to think of myself as a film director and make full use of cinematic techniques – special effects, long shots and close-ups.

You don't, of course, have to use all the things I've done on every page of your own comic strip – in fact, it's better to use special effects sparingly – but do try to avoid having all the panels looking exactly the same.

Adding speech

While some comic strips tell stories using pictures only, many strips use lettering and speech balloons to give the cartoons a 'soundtrack'. There is one very important rule to remember when you are planning your comic strip drawings: people usually read cartoons from left to right and top to bottom, so whatever you want people to see and read first in your comic strips must be on the left of your picture. The examples below show what happens when this rule is forgotten (see also pages 56-7).

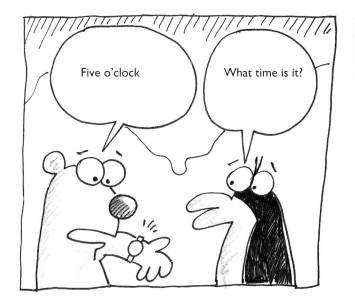

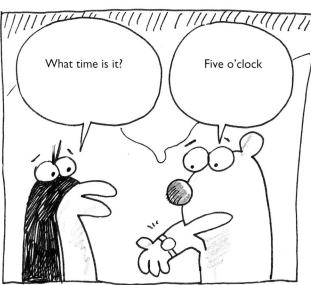

1 If you read this cartoon from left to right *(above left)*, the answer comes before the question.

2 One way of correcting this is simply to switch the characters around *(above)*.

3 Another solution is to put one balloon on top of the other *(left)*.

Speech Bubbles

Everyone knows that cartoon characters speak in 'bubbles' or 'balloons'. But, as your characters come to life, you'll want them to do a whole lot more than just speak – you may want them to shout, scream, or sing as well. Luckily, cartoonists have worked out their own 'sound effects' system. There are a whole range of special speech bubbles to show whether your characters are whispering, shouting, or just silently thinking to themselves. You can also use the balloons as another way of showing how your characters are feeling. Here, you can see some examples of how speech balloons can be used to 'add sound' to your cartoons.

Creating your own bubbles

If you have come up with some unusual characters of your own, perhaps you can design appropriate speech balloons to make them even more individual.

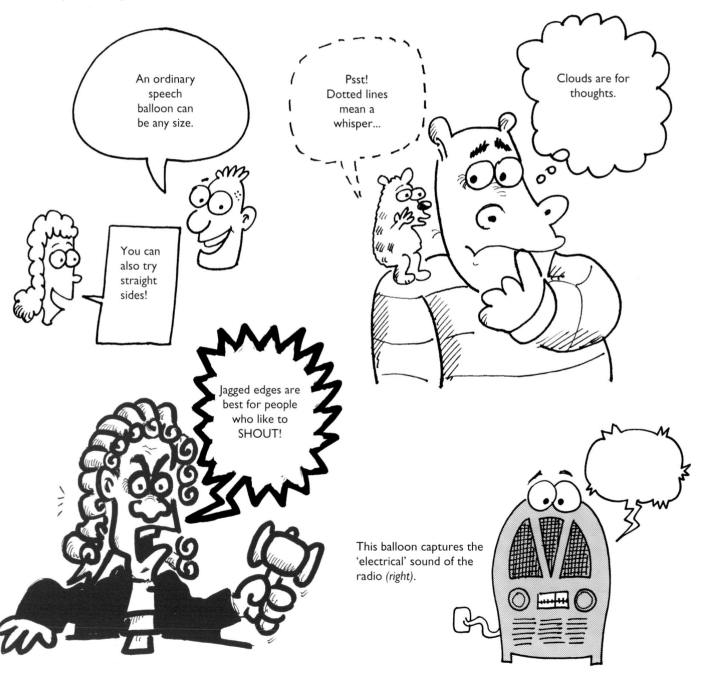

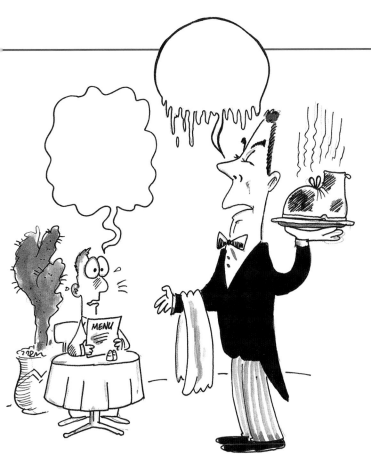

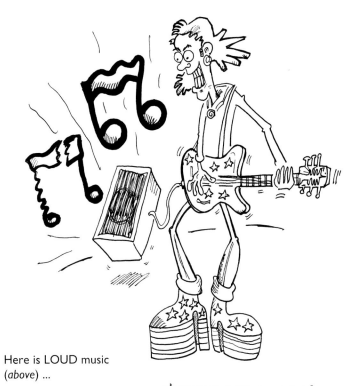

In this cartoon (*above*), the wavy lines on the diner's speech balloon make his words seem very weak and embarrassed. The waiter's balloon is perfect for saying something cold and unhelpful. What do you think they are saying to each other?

Here is LOUD music (*above*) ...

... and this is how to show that someone is saying something best left to the imagination (*left*)!

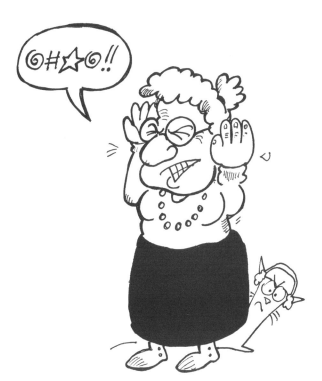

Lettering

Although a picture may be worth a thousand words, one or two words added to your cartoon drawings can make them work even better. In cartoons, you can use just as much imagination, energy and liveliness in drawing the lettering as in drawing the characters – and you don't need to worry too much about straight lines!

Styles of lettering

On these pages I've given some examples of some of the most popular types of lettering used in cartoons and comics, as well as some you could use for special occasions, or just for fun. Try writing your own name in some of the styles below or make up some styles of your own.

Keep it simple

As with drawings, simplicity works best for lettering – one or two special effects on every page is more than enough! Remember that no matter how wild or exaggerated the lettering style you choose for your cartoons, lettering works best when it's still possible to read it.

Always sketch your letters out roughly first to make sure they will fit your cartoon, and remember to check your spelling – when you're working on each letter one by one it's very easy to get them in the wrong order.

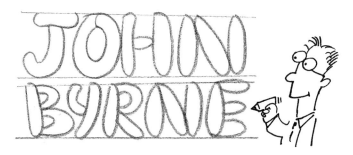

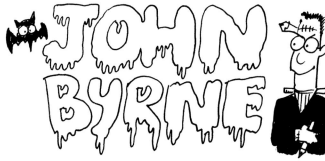

1 You can build up your cartoon letters from basic shapes, exactly as you do with your characters. Start off by pencilling in some ovals. You can 'bend' the letters when necessary and the top and bottom guidelines will still keep everything straight.

'Dripping' letters are very handy when you want to tell a horror story ... just make sure that they don't drip so much that you can't make out what they are (*above*). When you have inked the letters in, rub out the pencilled guidelines underneath.

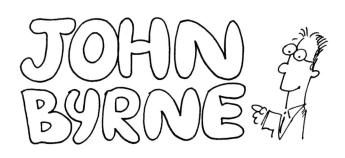

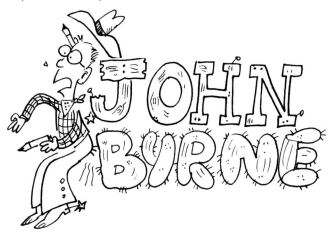

2 Now you can complete the letter shapes in darker pen. Rub out the guidelines to finish off.

For a Western, the letters can be made out of wood ... or cactus (*above*).

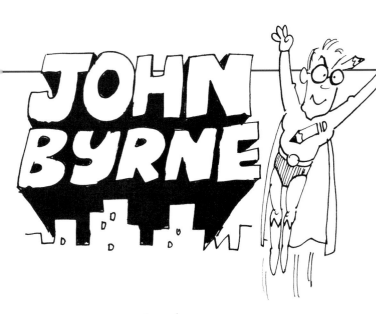

Big block letters with lots of shadow mean that this is a job for Super-Cartoonist (*left*)!

A 'dropped shadow' behind your letters makes them seem to float above the page (*below*).

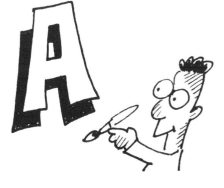

A little snow on top of a letter creates a seasonal effect (*below*).

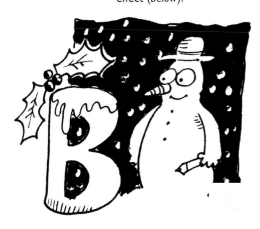

Drawing a flash and adding a few stars behind your letters is good for magic ... or superhero punches (*above*).

When you've finished lettering all your cartoon drawings, you can turn the letters themselves into cartoons (*below*).

You can also try replacing one of the letters in your word with a suitable

drawing – snakes are particularly obliging animals for this (*above*).

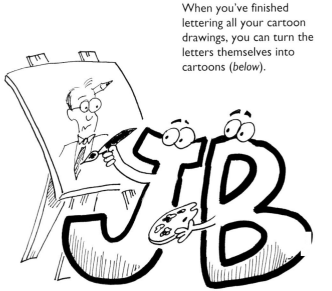

Using your Sketchbook

Cartoon ideas can come from anywhere. Buy yourself a small sketchbook or notebook, and carry it everywhere. An ordinary pencil or ball-point pen is fine for sketching.

Finding your subjects
Keep an eye out for interesting people who can become your cartoon characters. You'll find lots of subjects on the street, in restaurants, or on trains and buses. You'll soon get in the habit of doing quick sketches of people you meet – you'll have to be quick because your models are not going to stay in one place for very long.

Don't be too shy about cartooning in public. Some artists are a bit reluctant to let the public see them at work in case they get funny looks. But being funny is what cartooning is all about, and you'll usually find people are too busy laughing at your cartoons to bother laughing at you. Keep practising and it won't be too long before someone looks over your shoulder and says, 'I wish I could do that.'

If you prefer, you needn't even step outside your house to practise sketching. You'll find lots of funny things to draw in pictures from newspapers and magazines or people you draw from the television.

Quick technique
You'll find the same 'basic shapes' techniques we have used in cartooning just as useful in sketching real people. Concentrate on getting a quick, overall picture of the person, paying special attention to any interesting physical features or clothes to use in your cartoons.

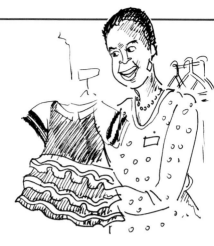

I sketched this woman at work in a clothes shop ...

... and invented a difficult customer for her. The caption might read: 'Sorry madam – I don't think we have it in size 200.'

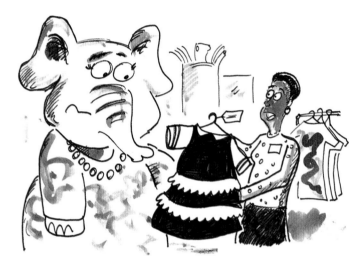

1 I saw this man while I was standing in the rain.

2 I didn't have an umbrella so I used the cartoon to take a little harmless revenge.

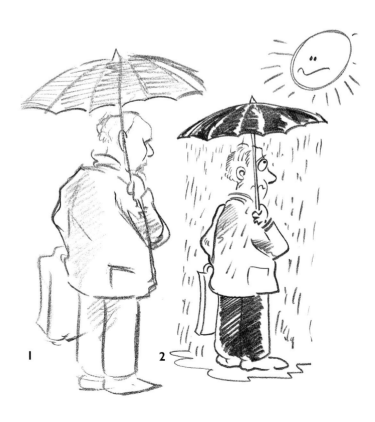

1

2

Using your sketches

Among the drawings on these pages, you will see some sketches from a shopping trip to my local town and the cartoons I turned them into when I got home.

One good way to make a cartoon is to choose two sketches you have done of different people and see what would happen if you put them together. Another trick is to sketch a person and then turn them into the cartoon animal you think they resemble. You can also try sketching everyday situations and then asking yourself what could happen next to make a funny cartoon.

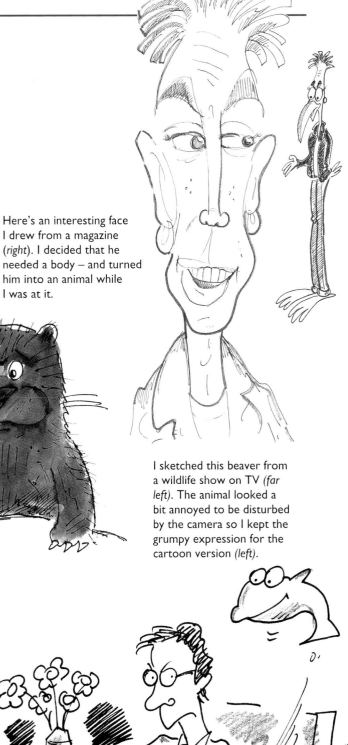

Here's an interesting face I drew from a magazine *(right)*. I decided that he needed a body – and turned him into an animal while I was at it.

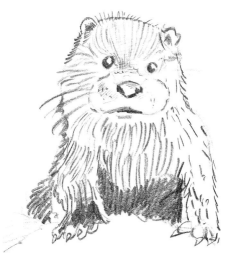

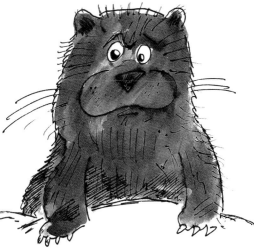

I sketched this beaver from a wildlife show on TV *(far left)*. The animal looked a bit annoyed to be disturbed by the camera so I kept the grumpy expression for the cartoon version *(left)*.

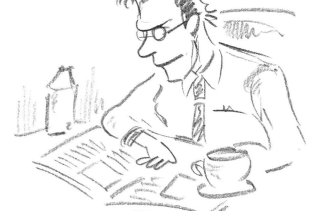

1 I spotted this poor chap in a cafe enjoying a nice quiet cup of coffee ...

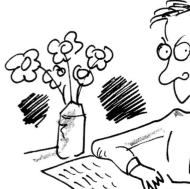

2 ... but nobody relaxes for long when there's a cartoonist about!

Using your Cartoons

This book is just the beginning of your cartoon adventure. As you keep practising your cartooning skills, your work will continue to improve, and you'll come up with lots of new ideas. You'll also come up with lots of new ways to use your cartoons. You'll certainly never be at a loss for interesting gifts to amuse your family and friends.

Earlier in this book we looked at some of the different drawing media from pen and ink to brush and crayon. We've also looked at the effects of drawing on different types of paper. But when you are thinking of ways to use your cartoons, there is only one basic rule you have to remember: if you can make a mark with something, you can draw a cartoon with it, and if anything stands still long enough you can draw a cartoon of it! On these pages I've suggested a few ways to put your cartoons to work – but with a little imagination, you will be able to come up with lots more.

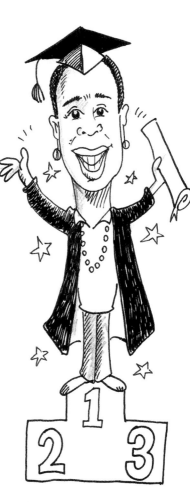

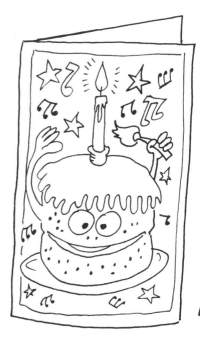

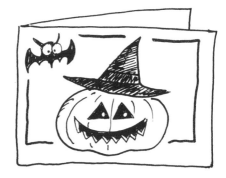

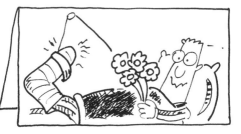

Holidays, birthdays, get well soon – there are lots of cartoon characters to suit every occasion *(left* and *below)*.

On special occasions such as graduation day, your greeting will be even more effective if you use your caricature skills to make the character on the card look like the person you are sending it to *(above)*.

Greetings cards

Finding appropriate greetings cards for friends and family can often be a problem. Not any more – now you can produce them yourself. There are lots of attractive coloured cards and papers available for you to use.

T-shirts

You can make your own T-shirts by painting cartoons on to them with fabric paints or waterproof markers. It makes drawing easier if you pin the front of the shirt on to a sheet of stiff cardboard while you are drawing. If you like, you can draw your preliminary sketch lightly with chalk.

Letters and notes

Notes and letters with cartoons are guaranteed to get noticed. Now that you are a cartoonist, why not design your own notepaper? A simple design works best and is easy and cheap to print or photocopy.

Animation

Making animated cartoons can be an expensive and complicated business – it takes 24 different drawings to make every second of film! But you can animate your drawings very simply by using the technique shown below.

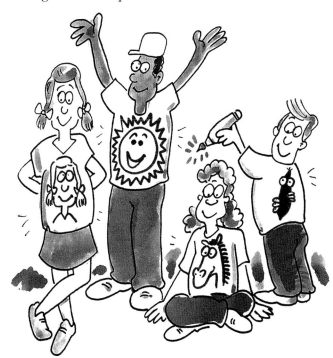

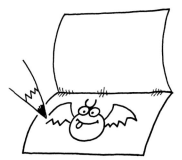

You can bind some photocopied cartoons together to make a notebook *(left)*.

Big, simple designs work best for T-shirt decoration, and are much easier to draw on the fabric *(right)*.

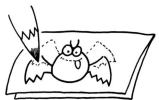

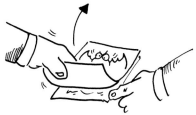

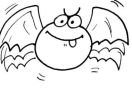

1 Fold a sheet of paper in two and draw a simple cartoon on the bottom half.

2 Fold the top half down and trace the cartoon exactly, but change one or two things. In this example, the position of the wings and tongue have been changed.

3 & 4 When you flip the top page quickly back and forth, your cartoon will appear to move. Now try a different 'cartoon movie' of your own!

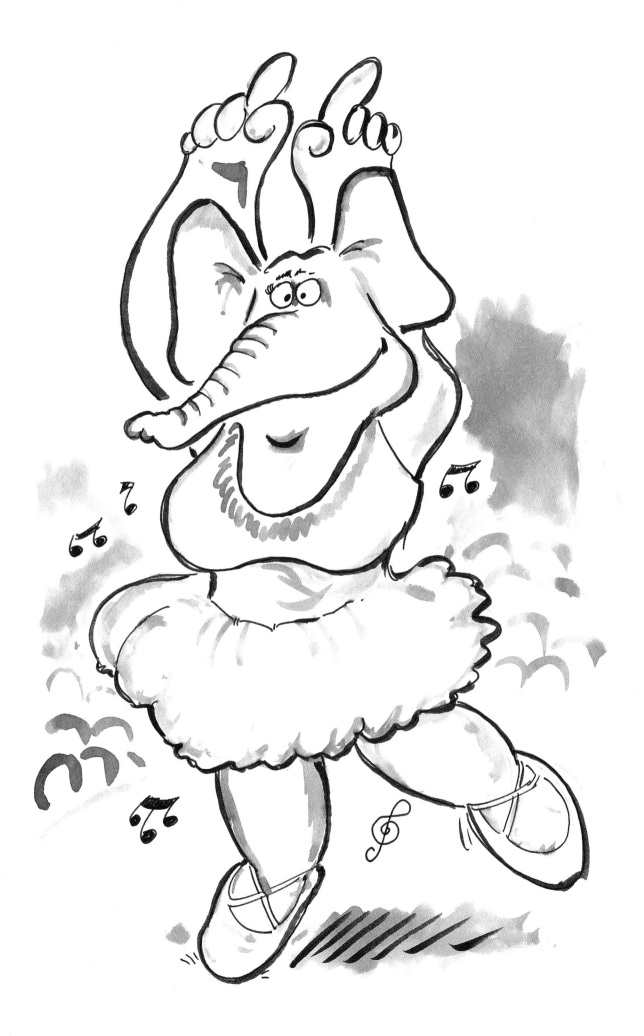